The Warning, Consolation, and Miracle in 2016

The Warning, Consolation, and Miracle in 2016

by
Ronald L. Conte Jr.

"Take care not to be disturbed.
For these things must be,
but the end is not so soon."
(Matthew 24:6)

The Warning, Consolation, and Miracle in 2016

Written, edited, and published by:
Ronald L. Conte Jr.

Copyright 2007, 2009, 2010, 2012, 2014.

Quotations from Sacred Scripture are from
the Catholic Public Domain Version of the Bible,
translated, edited, and published by Ronald L. Conte Jr.

First publication of this edition: December 4th, 2014.

Table of Contents

Cast of Spring by T. C. Murray, July, 1958
Pajoe Rooney, Dilly Morrissey, Tommy Fahy
Leonora Fahy, Tommy Fahy, Miriam Dooley

46

PARISH MEDIA

This article appeared in the May 1981 issue of Intercom) Newsletters, weekly or monthly or just occasionally, now play a very important role. Some are just a foolscap sheet reproduced on a duplicator. Some use a printed heading and form pages of print. Some use a readymade onside page with local news and reproduce inside. Otheruse offset. Some use colour. It does not matter in the end for the real test of a newsletter is the extent to which it influences local attitudes and breaks prejudices. A parish annual or quarterly usually with a strong interest in local history of which THE BLAZER from Craughwell is a good example, is particularly popular with emigrants.

This is the story of one parish magazine produced in a rural parish of 260 families and 1,100 souls. First issued in 1975, the publication has to date run to nine numbers. It was hoped to produce a number each quarter but this was found to be impractical owing to the amount of work involved. It is now produced annually and it has 84pages of closely printed material selling at 80p per copy. It includes photos but there are no advertisements.

In spite of the small population there is a circulation of over 1,000 copies, about four copies per house. The extra copies go to friends and relatives scattered to the four corners of the earth. Local shopkeepers handle all sales without profit. Practically all the writing is done by the priests and people of the parish. The magazine tries to be homely and unpretentious.

In this way a rural parish is turned into the centre of the world for its own people. Seeking writers during pastoral visitation has proved useful, for those visited are often eager to discusst the magazine and its contents. In a few cases writers of some talent have been discovered among the ordinary people.

In one case the sixty-five year old wife of a farmer has shown remarkable talent for comment and comedy. A farmer and an industrial worker both with natural literary skills have had the great satisfaction of seeing them writing in print. Now are separated brethren in the parish forgotten. They take a keen interest in the magazine and one Church of Ireland neighbour contributed a most interesting article. Contributions cover a wide variety of interests: the church, parish history, extracts from parish records, reports from parish societies, parish sports, news old and new, folklore, poetry, ballads, letters, travel, placenames, agriculture, etc. It takes about two months of fairly constant work to put the magazine together.

It is more than worth the effort, judging from the reaction of the readers, understandably it pleases the exiles and those who once lived in the parish, and many readers generously send honations to ensure that lack of money should not prevent publication. So fortunatley in spite of rising printing costs, our credit balance is healthy. Each succeeding issue is enthusiastically welcomed not alone in the home parish but also in the surrounding parishes. And now three neighbouring parishes have launched their own parish annuals.

Inevitably the editor does fair a share of the writing. There is no supporting local committee which is probably a fault. However the present arrangement leaves the editor totally free to get on with the work.

Since knowledge and awareness of each others helps to knit the members of a community together, the magazine is a unifying agent in the parish. It creates community and helps to strengthen parochial identity. It helps to strengthen people's "roots".

Introduction

I have never received any private revelations myself. I have not had any conversations or communications about the secrets with any of the visionaries of Medjugorje or Garabandal. This book about the secrets is my own personal understanding, based on what is already publicly known about the secrets, and based on my interpretation of the Bible as well as my study of Catholic eschatology over the course of many years.

I only write what I sincerely believe to be true. But I am fallible, so the future may be somewhat different than what I have written. I know that this book may be controversial, especially among devotees of Medjugorje and Garabandal. But I believe that the dates and events of the future can be understood, to a limited extent, through the study of eschatology. As always, my work in eschatology is speculative and fallible. The reader should consider my writings on this topic to be speculative opinion, not dogma or doctrine.

My work in eschatology began in the mid-1990's. My first book of theology was a work of eschatology, titled "The Bible and the Future", and published in 1998. The last chapter of that book contained my interpretation of passages from Scripture referring to the Warning and Miracle of Garabandal. Subsequent editions of that book, eventually retitled as "The Bible and the Future of the World", were more specific about the events of the Warning and Miracle. So my writings and insights on this subject go back many years.

My published work in eschatology, currently in print as of this writing, includes the following books:

* Apocalypse Survival Guide for Christians
* The Bible and the Future: 2013 Edition
* The First Part of the Tribulation
* The Second Part of the Tribulation

* The Secrets of La Salette and the End Times
* The Secrets of Medjugorje and Garabandal Revealed
* On World War 3 and World War 4
* Eschatological Commentary on the Apocalypse of John
* Eschatological Commentary on the Four Gospels

and the following booklets:

* The Great Catholic Monarch and the Angelic Shepherd
* The Three Days of Darkness and the Time of Peace
* The Kingdom of the Ten Kings
* The Return of Jesus Christ
as well as the present title.

In addition, I have written several works of Roman Catholic moral theology, including: The Catechism of Catholic Ethics, Roman Catholic Marital Sexual Ethics, Roman Catholic Teaching on Abortion and Contraception, and Is Lying Always Wrong? My other writings cover the topics of Biblical chronology, Mariology, theology of the Trinity, and salvation theology.

My work with the Bible includes a new translation of Sacred Scripture. I translated the entire Latin Vulgate Bible into English, using the Challoner Douay text as a guide. My work on this new translation began in mid-March of 2004, and was completed in late March of 2009. I worked on this translation of the Bible nearly every day for five years. And when it was completed, I placed the entire work in the public domain, so that no one would own the translation, and it could be used, published, and updated by any of the faithful. The translation is called: The Catholic Public Domain Version of the Sacred Bible (CPDV). It is available for free online on my Bible website: www.SacredBible.org

Other authors write in the field of Roman Catholic eschatology. But they are usually not theologians who have researched and written on other topics, such as dogmatic or moral theology. And their work in Biblical studies is often lacking. Of greater concern is the fact that some authors make use of doubtful or discredited sources in their eschatology, including disreputable claimed private revelations. A few even claim to have received private revelation themselves, on which their eschatology is supposedly based.

I caution the reader not to be too quick to believe anything asserted in the field of eschatology. As for my writings, I present my work in eschatology as a type of fallible speculative theology. But I notice that many other authors do not do the same. So I'm concerned that, once the tribulation begins, many souls will be led astray by authors whose writings in eschatology include doctrinal claims that are false, harmful, or even heretical. What you may want to look for in an author of eschatology is a sound understanding of dogma and doctrine on a range of subjects in theology, and prudence in evaluating non-dogmatic sources.

I suggest avoiding any author or book making any of the following claims: that the Antichrist is in the world today, that Jesus will return for this generation, that the Pope will go astray or commit heresy or become a false prophet or become the Antichrist, or any similar claim that undermines the one holy Catholic Church. Another common false claim in eschatology is the idea that the Church is under attack by "freemasonry", or "illuminati", or other types of conspiracy theories. I would also avoid any eschatology that describes the tribulation as being, in any substantial way, a result of global warming, or pollution, or extreme weather. The Bible contains many passages of eschatology, and the Saints have also written much on this subject, thereby proving that such claims are not tenable.

I am very concerned that, when the Warning from God happens, people will believe to be credible anyone who gave the correct date in advance or who wrote about the topic. Be advised that more than a few false private revelations use the technique of taking information from true private revelations, such as the Warning and the Miracle of Garabandal, in order to make their own claims of private revelation seem true. Then there are incompetent authors, who compile every possible claim in eschatology, and those whose judgment in matters of theology is untrustworthy. I suppose that, ultimately, the reader must decide whom to trust. Be cautious. Do not believe every claim.

Already, I find many false claims being spread online and in print about Roman Catholic eschatology, about the future of the Church, and about the Warning, Miracle, and other events. You can always trust the teaching of the Pope, and the teaching of the body of Bishops who remain in communion with each successive Pope. You should always reject any person or group claiming that the Pope or the body of Bishops has gone astray. And avoid anyone who exalts private revelation above the Divine Revelation of Sacred Tradition and Sacred Scripture, or above the teaching authority of the one true Church (the Magisterium).

May God give you grace and peace in the difficult years ahead.

1. The Warning of Garabandal

Please understand that my writings about the future are speculative eschatology, based on study and interpretation, not based on knowledge that is absolute or certain.

The Timing of the Warning

Year: 2016
Month and day: March 25th
Liturgical Calendar: Good Friday

Time of Day: The same time that Jesus died on the Cross, which is about the ninth hour (cf. Mark 15:33) Jerusalem sun time, which is about 2:51 p.m. Israel Standard Time (IST). Since the Warning occurs everywhere at the same moment, the time on the clock will vary by time zone: 2:51 p.m. IST is 12:51 UTC (Universal Coordinated Time), which is 8:51 a.m. on the East coast of the United States (Eastern Daylight Time).

It is interesting to note that March 25th is usually the solemnity of the Annunciation, when the Incarnation was announced to Mary, but not when it coincides with Good Friday.

Introduction

The secrets of Medjugorje and Garabandal foretell a set of events which will be important to the life of the Church. The visionaries at both apparition sites describe these secrets as having dramatic and serious consequences for the whole world. I believe, furthermore, that these events will become a fundamental part of the history of salvation. Therefore, these events cannot be found solely in private revelation. For nothing so important to salvation can be absent from Sacred Tradition and Sacred Scripture. And if this is so, then these events must be described in some manner, either explicitly or implicitly, in Sacred Scripture. By studying Scripture, then, we can know what the secrets are, in advance of their unfolding.

[Zechariah]
{12:10} And I will pour out upon the house of David and upon the inhabitants of Jerusalem, the spirit of grace and of prayers. And they will look upon me, whom they have pierced, and they will mourn for him as one mourns for an only son, and they will feel sorrow over him, as one would be sorrowful at the death of a firstborn.

In one sense, this passage refers to the Crucifixion. But the details of the passage and especially the whole chapter are not a close fit for that event. Some other event seems to be indicated. This should not be surprising, since many passages in Scripture have more than one meaning intended by God.

In my interpretation, this passage of Scripture refers to the Warning of Garabandal. On the day of the Warning, God pours out a spirit of repentance from sin, and the faithful will mourn over their sins and over the harm done by their sins. Some very faithful souls will also share in the sorrow that Christ felt on the Cross for the sinfulness of humanity. It will be like the sorrow of the death of a firstborn son. During this event, the Church will sorrow over the death of the firstborn Son of God, Jesus, and over all the sins of the world for which He died.

Notice that this mourning is a result of the spirit of grace and prayer poured out on the people, and also a result of considering Christ on the Cross: "they will look upon me, whom they have pierced...." (Zech 12:10). The Warning is a day of repentance worldwide. But all true repentance occurs in cooperation with grace, and so all true repentance is a fruit from the tree of the Cross. Therefore, this event of the Warning, this special and singular day when God enlightens and prompts the consciences of each and every human person on earth at the same time, is a gift from Christ on the Cross. Therefore also, the most fitting day for this event is Good Friday.

By placing this event on Good Friday, God is indicating to the whole world that the Christian Faith is the source of true knowledge about morals, sin, and salvation in Christ Jesus. If this event were to occur on some other day, a day not strongly associated with the liturgical calendar, then some persons would likely turn this event into its own religion. They would be led away from the Church and away from Christ. And so God wisely places this event on a day that will signal to the whole world that they should follow Christ and His Church. For He is the only source of salvation from sin, and the one true Church is the only Ark of that very same salvation.

When the Warning occurs in 2016, the date of Good Friday will coincide with the usual day for the celebration of the Incarnation of Christ (the solemnity of the Annunciation). This coincidence is fitting, for our salvation is from Christ on the Cross because He is God incarnate.

The poet John Donne expressed this connection between the Incarnation and the Crucifixion in a profound and succinct manner in his poem:

Upon The Annunciation and Passion
Falling Upon One Day.
(March 25th, 1608)

Tamely, frail body, abstain today; today
My soul eats twice, Christ hither and away.

She sees Him man, so like God made in this,
That of them both a circle emblem is,
Whose first and last concur; this doubtful day
Of feast or fast, Christ came, and went away.

She sees Him nothing, twice at once, who's all;
She sees a Cedar plant itself, and fall;
Her Maker put to making, and the Head
Of life, at once, not yet alive, yet dead.

3

She sees at once the Virgin Mother stay
Reclused at home, public at Golgotha;
Sad and rejoiced she's seen at once, and seen
At almost fifty, and at scarce fifteen.

At once a Son is promised her, and gone;
Gabriel gives Christ to her, He her to John;
Not fully a mother, She's in orbity [*in grief*];
At once receiver and the legacy.

All this, and all between, this day hath shown,
Th'abridgement of Christ's story, which makes one --
As in plain maps, the furthest west is east --
Of th'angels Ave, and Consummatum est.

How well the Church, God's Court of Faculties
Deals, in sometimes, and seldom joining these!

As by the self-fix'd Pole we never do
Direct our course, but the next star thereto,
Which shows where th'other is, and which we say
-- Because it strays not far -- doth never stray;

So God by His Church, nearest to Him, we know
And stand firm, if we by her motion go;
His Spirit, as His fiery pillar, doth
Lead, and His Church, as cloud; to one end both.

This Church, by letting those days join, hath shown
Death and conception in mankind is one;
Or 'twas in Him the same humility,
That He would be a man, and leave to be;

Or as creation He hath made, as God,
With the last judgment, but one period,
His imitating Spouse would join in one
Manhood's extremes: He shall come, He is gone;

4

Or as though one blood drop, which thence did fall,
Accepted, would have served, He yet shed all,
So though the least of His pains, deeds, or words,
Would busy a life, she all this day affords;

This treasure then, in gross, my soul, up-lay,
And in my life retell it every day.

-- by John Donne

The Warning: Why will it happen?

The purpose of the Warning is not merely to correct sinners for their sins. The people of every generation since the fall of Adam and Eve have been sinners. And yet this unique event did not occur in any past generation. So why does God give the world this particular gift at this particular time? His purpose is to strengthen and guide us during the first part of the tribulation.

I've gone back and forth in my opinion as to the timing of the tribulation in relation to the Warning, especially whether the Warning would occur before or after the start of the tribulation. It is possible for the tribulation to begin in 2015, with the Warning as one of the early events of that whole time period. But presently I consider it most likely that the tribulation will begin very soon after the Warning, Consolation, and Miracle in 2016.

In order to prepare the world and the Church for the very severe set of afflictions which occur during the tribulation, God begins by giving the world three special blessings. These blessings are the first three secrets of Medjugorje. I believe that the first secret of Medjugorje is the same as the Warning of Garabandal, and the third secret of Medjugorje is the same as the Miracle of Garabandal. The second secret of Medjugorje is an event not mentioned at Garabandal, which I term "the Consolation". Each of these three events is intended by God to strengthen the human person.

The first event, the Warning, blesses and strengthens the human soul by showing each person all the sins still remaining on their conscience, and by offering the gift of repentance from sin. The second event is a day of supernatural Consolation of the human spirit (the mind and heart), given only to those who repented on the day of the Warning. The third event is the Miracle of Garabandal, which includes very many miraculous healings of the body for the benefit of repentant persons around the world.

But these three great blessings are not an indication that a time of peace is about to begin. Far from it. This threefold gift is strength for the journey, an arduous and frightful journey, through the years of the first part of the tribulation. This supernatural strengthening is necessary because the events of the tribulation are more terrible than can be imagined. Without these three blessings, many more souls would be lost.

The visionaries of Garabandal have said that the Warning will occur when things are at their worst. When they were each young girls (about 11 or 12 years of age), they saw a set of visions of the future. They concluded from those images that these events will occur in a particular order. Perhaps they erred in their understanding of the vision they were shown, to some extent, at least concerning the order of events.

But what I consider to be more likely is that things will be "at their worst" in terms of sinfulness prior to the tribulation. If the Warning and Miracle precede (by a few weeks or months) the tribulation, then those events should increase the holiness of the faithful and thereby improve the situation of the world from a spiritual point of view. Things will be worse, spiritually, before the Warning, and somewhat better afterward. But in a worldly sense, things become worse and worse as the afflictions of the tribulation progress, for one suffering follows another.

Thus, after the first few years of the tribulation unfold, God gives the whole world the Warning, as an opportunity to repent from

past sins, as an opportunity for sinners to change the cour
their lives. For the tribulation only occurs due to the unrepenta
sins of humanity. At the Warning, God allows humanity tu
reassess its course. If everyone repents, then the tribulation would
not occur -- but such will not be the case. We know from infallible
Sacred Scripture that the tribulation will happen. Even so, God is
just and merciful, and so He gives us the opportunity to be spared
from the tribulation, even though He knows that far too many
persons will reject the offer to repent.

On the other hand, many faithful souls will accept the gift of the
Warning, and will sincerely and thoroughly repent from their sins.
Persons who repent and reform their lives will suffer much less
during the tribulation than those who either refuse to repent, or
who repent and then relapse. As I see it, one of the purposes of the
Warning in the plan of God is to lessen the sufferings of the
tribulation. **The repentance of millions of souls reduces the
severity of the tribulation, because the tribulation is a
punishment from God for sin, especially unrepentant grave sin.**
The Warning brings many to repentance, resulting in less suffering
than there would otherwise be.

The Warning: When will it happen?

I believe that the Warning must occur soon. There are many
reasons for this conclusion. Generally speaking, the Warning is
inextricably linked to the start of the tribulation. But the reasons
why the tribulation must occur soon are too many and too
complex for this book. I'll summarize those reasons below, but for
the full explanation, see my two book set: *The First Part of the
Tribulation* and *The Second Part of the Tribulation*.

My opinions in eschatology are speculative and fallible, but they
are not without a firm basis. I have been studying and writing
eschatology for nearly 20 years now (since the mid-1990's). My
stated specific reasons for a conclusion in eschatology should
always be understood to include the more general basis of many
years studying the field.

inion in Roman Catholic eschatology, which I
.e tribulation is divided into two parts. The first
.oulation is called the "lesser tribulation", and the
. is called the "greater tribulation". In my view, the first
.rs for this generation (early 21st century), and then there
.ng respite before the second part of the tribulation begins in
. early 25th century. Though the tribulation begins soon, it will
not be completed until hundreds of years in the future. Recall the
words of our Savior: "Take care not to be disturbed. For these
things must be, but the end is not so soon." (Mt 24:6).

What is the basis for my belief that the first part of the tribulation
occurs soon? There are many reasons. I will mention only a few of
the highlights here. First, I've identified two eschatological figures
mentioned frequently in the eschatology of Catholics Saints: the
Angelic Shepherd and the great Catholic monarch. I believe that
Fr. Zlatko Sudac of Krk island is the Angelic Shepherd. He has a
miraculous sign of the cross on his forehead, and he has
miraculous abilities, including bi-location. He is the future Pope
Raphael, the Pope in red who guides the Church during the worst
years of the tribulation. And I believe that the great Catholic
monarch is Ferdinand Zvonimir von Hapsburg, rightful heir to the
Austrian empire and to the holy Roman empire. These two
persons are in the world today. Father Sudac is in his adult years,
and Ferdinand is in his teens (b. 1997).

A number of prophecies place these two figures in power, the
Angelic Shepherd as a future Pope and the great Catholic
monarch as a future political leader, in the last years of the lesser
tribulation (the first part of the tribulation). So the start of the
tribulation cannot be far away.

My understanding is that two world wars are included in the first
part of the tribulation: World War 3, which is the first of the
Seven Seals in the Book of Revelation, and World War 4, which is
the sixth Seal. Each war is an exceedingly bloody conflict between
the Arab/Muslim nations of the Middle East and northern Africa,

led by extremists, and the Western nations, especially the United States and Europe. As you undoubtedly know from news stories in recent years, a conflict is building between Muslim extremists and the West. You might also be aware that Iran seems to be working toward the manufacture of weapon-grade uranium and nuclear bombs. Events are moving rather quickly now toward a major war in Europe. And there are specific Catholic prophecies, remarkably from many years ago, about a conflict between Muslim extremists and the West as part of the events of the tribulation.

Then there is a spiritual basis for believing the tribulation to be near: the increasing sinfulness of the world and the progression in the Church toward a schism. The great apostasy is an event predicted by Sacred Scripture to occur during the end times (2 Thess 2:3-8). More on that event later in this book. My point here is that the situation of the Church on earth at the present time indicates that the apostasy is near.

Most persons who call themselves Catholics do not practice the faith, or they barely practice it. Most Catholics who go to Mass do not go to Confession. Most who claim to be believing and practicing Catholics do not accept teaching and correction from the Pope and the body of Bishops. They believe whatever they like. Most liberal Catholics believe whatever ideas are prevalent in sinful secular society at the moment. Most conservative Catholics believe whatever ideas are prevalent in the conservative subculture, even if those ideas contradict magisterial teaching. And the traditionalists have decided that they alone determine what is and is not true doctrine and sound discipline.

Certainly, a person can be liberal and orthodox, or conservative and orthodox. And there are some traditionalists who remain faithful to every teaching of the Magisterium, even those teachings that are (or seem to be) liberal. But most Catholics reject the role of the Pope to teach and correct. If the Pope says anything, on any topic, contrary to their own thinking, they automatically assume that the Pope must be wrong. The sheer arrogance of this assumption is astounding. Truly, the foundation for the great apostasy has been laid.

For more details on the start of the tribulation and the events of its unfolding, see my other books of Catholic eschatology. The tribulation is about to begin, and the Warning is one of its first events, perhaps the very first event.

There are also some specific reasons, based on the messages of Garabandal, for my belief that the Warning occurs on Good Friday of 2016. As I've explained above, the day when we recall and celebrate the salvific suffering and death of our Savior, Jesus Christ, one of the holiest days of the year, Good Friday, is a fitting day for the event of the Warning. For that event is a call to accept the graces obtained for us on the Cross, especially the grace to repent from sin. No other day in the liturgical calendar is such a close fit for an event that I have termed "The Day of Repentance".

But which year holds the Good Friday of the Warning? As I will explain in detail in the chapter on the Miracle of Garabandal, the great Miracle occurs on the evening of May 12th in 2016. The Blessed Virgin Mary gave the visionaries of Garabandal some helpful hints so that some of the faithful might discern the dates of these events in advance. She said that the Miracle would occur in the evening, on a Thursday, on the feast day of a young martyr of the Eucharist, but not on a day that is a feast day for Jesus or Mary.

I've determined that day to be May 12th. But that calendar date does not usually fall on a Thursday. The years of that coincidence are: 2016, 2022, 2033, 2039, 2044. Given the ages of the Angelic Shepherd and the great Catholic monarch, and the nearness of World War 3, the last three dates listed above are easily ruled out. The date of 2022 is also, in all likelihood, too far into the future, given the nearness of the great apostasy and of World War 3. In addition, the "three Popes prophecy" by one of the visionaries of Garabandal indicates the earlier date.

The Miracle of Garabandal therefore falls on 12 May 2016, and the Warning occurs prior to that event, on Good Friday. You might suppose that the Warning could occur on Good Friday of 2015. However, the visionaries of Garabandal have said that the Miracle occurs less than a year after the Warning. May 12th of 2016 is more than a year after Good Friday of 2015. So that leaves only 2016 as the year for the Warning.

This conclusion as to the date of the Warning, Good Friday, March 25th, in 2016 is a result of my work in eschatology over the course of many years. I first proposed this date in 2013, and I have continued to assert it in my eschatology in print and online. Be advised that some persons have taken portions of my work in eschatology, including this date, to claim as if it were their own.

In addition, through my work in biblical chronology, I determined that the first Passover of Jesus' ministry was in spring of A.D. 16. Jesus was baptized in autumn of AD 15, and crucified in spring of AD 19. So the 2000th anniversary of the first Passover of Christ's Ministry occurs in 2016. At that first Passover of His Divine Ministry, Jesus purified the Temple by driving the buyers and sellers out of the Temple. Similarly, by means of the Warning on Good Friday of 2016, Jesus will purify the Church on earth by striking the conscience of all sinners on earth, including within the Church. Many great sinners will repent greatly. But then, too, many sinners will reject this correction, and thereby fall away from the Church as part of the continuation of the great apostasy.

The Three Popes Prophecy

One of the visionaries of Garabandal, named Conchita, has made an often repeated, and almost as often misstated, prediction -- that there would be three more Popes and then ... something. It is not clear, at first glance, what would happen after the reigns of three Popes. However, Conchita did explicitly state that it was not the end of the world.

On 3 June 1963 -- the day of the passing of Pope John
XXIII -- after learning that the village bells were tolling
for the pope, Conchita made a startling remark to her
mother Aniceta: "For sure...now there remain no more
than three [popes]!"

...

Naturally, Aniceta was shocked, and asked if this meant
the end of the world was approaching (¿Quiere decir que
viene ya el fin del mundo?). Conchita's response was that
the Virgin did not say "the end of the world", but rather
"the end of the times".

...

Specifically, the Virgin mentioned that there would be
two more popes after the then-current pontiff (Paul VI,
1963-1978), and then the end of the times.[1]

So the event that occurs after the reigns of three popes is
apparently the beginning of the end times, that is to say, the
beginning of the tribulation. But it is not the end of the world.

Note that the author of the above quoted article is the one stating
that the three popes must include Paul VI. But I can find no quote
from Conchita making such an assertion. So perhaps he made an
incorrect assumption that point.

Conchita made this prophecy after Pope Paul VI was elected. But
obviously, at the present time, we can assume that the count of
three popes does not include Paul VI. Otherwise, we would be
past the count of three. So the expression "three more" must refer
to the next three, after the pope in office at the time (Paul VI).
And that conclusion leaves us with the following list of the
subsequent 3 popes:

1. Pope John Paul I
2. Pope John Paul II
3. Pope Benedict XVI

The reign of Pope Benedict XVI ended with his valid resignation, but the end times have not begun. On the other hand, Pope Benedict is still alive. The prophecy could mean that the end times begin before Benedict XVI dies. Or we might interpret the "three more" popes expression to refer to the interim: Paul VI, then three popes, then the end times begin under that next Pope, who is Pope Francis. So the three popes represent the time period between the pope who had just been elected, when Conchita made the prophecy, and the pope during whose reign the tribulation begins. Either way, the start of the tribulation is very near.

Pope Francis himself has commented that his reign might only last a few years. When speaking to the news media, he suggested he would consider resigning, as Pope Benedict XVI did. Then he also said: "I know this will last a short time, two or three years, and then to the house of the Father."[2] By these words, he indicated that he might die and go to Heaven (the house of the Father) after not too many years as Pope.

As an aside: if Pope Francis does resign, that would leave us with an unusual situation: two validly resigned Popes and the next Pope in office, for a total of three Popes. The three popes prophecy does not state that there would be three popes alive at the same time, when the end times begin. But it is a possibility. Consider this passage from Sacred Scripture:

[Zechariah]
{11:8} And I cut down three shepherds in one month. And my soul became contracted concerning them, just as their soul also varied concerning me.

I have long interpreted the whole passage, from which this verse is taken, as having an eschatological meaning. Perhaps the three shepherds are two valid Popes who have resigned, but are still alive, plus the subsequent valid Pope: Pope Benedict XVI, Pope Francis, and his successor (Pope Pius XIII). If Pope Francis resigns, while Benedict XVI is still alive, it will be another clear indication that the end times are near.

But notice the implication of this prophecy from Scripture. God will "cut down three shepherds in one month", perhaps meaning that all three popes will die within about one month's time. This would further imply that the reigns of Pope Francis and his successor are each rather brief. (I've drawn this point from a brief discussion of the subject with members of my online group: CatholicPlanet.net)[3]

In any case, the idea that Pope Francis will have a short reign indicates that the start of the tribulation is near. It begins during his reign, most likely while Benedict XVI is still alive. And this is the specific fulfillment of the three popes prophecy. But this also suggests that the Warning of Garabandal occurs during the reign of Pope Francis. Thus, the 2016 date for the Warning is confirmed as correct, as other dates for that event would be too far in the future.

In the prophetic list of Popes given by St. Malachy, Pope Benedict is the next to last; he is called "The glory of the olive."[4] I interpret this saying to mean that he is a Pope of peace-making, prior to a severe war (the first Seal). So the war does not begin until after his reign ends. And this suggests that the Warning occurs after his reign and before the tribulation (the first affliction of which is war). The events of the Warning, Consolation, and Miracle are events of peace and holiness and blessing (but they will be terrifying to the sinful). They are followed by war because not enough persons repent, and too many fall back into sin after repentance.

Who is Peter the Roman?

While we are speaking of Popes, I would like to assert my current understanding of the prophecy of the popes of Saint Malachy. His prophetic list of popes ends with one called "Peter the Roman". And it might seem that Pope Francis is that pope, since his reign follows after Pope Benedict XVI, who fits the prophetic description of the next to last pope on the list, the one just before

Peter the Roman. But I have a different interpretation than most persons on that point.

Here is what St. Malachy said about Peter the Roman:

> "In the final persecution of the Holy Roman Church there shall reign Peter the Roman who will feed his flock amid many tribulations, after which the seven-hilled city will be destroyed and the terrible judge will judge the people."[5]

Though Peter the Roman is the last pope on the list, he does NOT represent the last pope ever. The description quoted above refers to the tribulation. But the tribulation unfolds in two parts, with an inter-tribulation period between, over a period of a few hundred years.

The "seven-hilled city" is Rome. So this prophecy is saying that Rome will be destroyed during the tribulation. But as the tribulation has two parts, we need not assume that the complete destruction of Rome is in the near future. I go into some detail on the future of Rome in my books *The First Part of the Tribulation* and *The Second Part of the Tribulation*. In this book, let me summarize. Rome will be struck by a nuclear missile during World War 3, as one of the early events during the invasion of Europe by the Muslim extremists. Note that Iran is presently (2014) close to obtaining weapon-grade uranium for a nuke. But that attack on Rome is not the end of the city. After the war, it is rebuilt. Then, hundreds of years later, during the second part of the tribulation, the city of Rome is again devastated in war. So the two-part tribulation sees two destructions of Rome, one for each part.

The term "Peter" in "Peter the Roman" refers to the office of the Pope, since every valid Pope is a successor of the Apostle Peter. The term "Roman" refers to the office of the Pope, since every valid Pope is the Bishop of Rome and the head of the Roman Catholic Church. Peter the Roman will "feed his flock", which is the role of every Pope.

So then, which pope, during the tribulation, is called "Peter the Roman"? All of them. In my interpretation, the expression "Peter the Roman" refers to every pope, from the pope who reigns at the start of the tribulation (Pope Francis) through all the popes who follow after him during the first part of the tribulation, and the inter-tribulation period, until the last pope before the Return of Jesus Christ. And that last pope before the Return reigns in the early 25th century. So Peter the Roman is not any one pope, but all the popes from now until Christ returns, at the end of the tribulation, in the distant future.

Events Before the Warning

As I write these words in November of 2014 (updating my writings on this topic which go back many years), the Warning on Good Friday of 2016 is a year and a few months away. What will happen between now and then? My answer is based on my years of study of Catholic eschatology.

Before the Warning: a Prelude to the Great Apostasy

The tribulation includes an event called the great apostasy. And since the tribulation is divided into two parts, each part experiences a great apostasy, a great falling away from the true Faith of Catholic Christianity. But before we discuss some of the details of that event, I want you to know that, as an article of faith infallibly taught by the ordinary and universal Magisterium:

The one holy Catholic Church is indefectible. She can never go astray from the true Faith and the path of salvation. She can never be taken over by evil leaders, nor fall under the control of the devil. For the gates of Hell cannot prevail against Her.

And the Roman Pontiff, the Pope of the Catholic Church, can never fall into heresy. The grace and providence of God absolutely prevents any Pope from committing the sin of heresy, or the sin of schism, or the sin of apostasy, because he is the head of the

Church, and the Church is indefectible. Even the body of Bishops, who remain in communion with the Pope, are prevented by the grace of God from committing apostasy, heresy, or schism as a body. An individual Bishop or a small group of Bishops can break away from the main body of Bishops and from the Pope, committing the grave sins of heresy and schism. But the Pope and the body of Bishops who remain in communion with him cannot fall into those sins. The grace of God preserves the indefectibility of the Church by securing their faith.

The great apostasy was mentioned by Jesus in his eschatological discourse:

[Matthew]
{24:4} And answering, Jesus said to them: "Pay attention, lest someone lead you astray.
{24:5} For many will come in my name saying, 'I am the Christ.' And they will lead many astray.

Many will come forward, as the tribulation unfolds, to lead astray the weak in faith, the foolish, and the unrepentant. Some will claim that their ideas are of Christ, as if they have come in His name to speak for Him. They are not of Christ; they are speaking against the teachings of Jesus and His Church. Some will claim to have receive private revelations from Christ and Mary. They have not received true private revelation from Heaven; their claimed private revelations are from fallen angels. And if anyone claims that Christ is returning for the present-day generation, do not believe it. Jesus will not return until all that is predicted in Sacred Scripture about the future of the Church and the world is fulfilled, and that set of events occupies many generations.

During the tribulation, fear of death and fear at the realization that the end times have begun will cause many sinners to grasp at straws, so to speak, by seeking any teacher or prophet who will reassure them. Many wicked persons will pose as holy persons, attempting to gain an audience; they will lead many astray. Do not be quick to believe any claim of private revelation. And take care to reject any visionary or teacher or leader whose words are contrary to the teachings of Jesus and His Church, the one holy Church led by each successor of Peter, that is to say, each valid Pope. There are many false claims of private revelation in the world today. "Pay attention, lest someone lead you astray." (Mt 24:4).

The great apostasy, during the first part of the tribulation, results in most Catholic laypersons, many priests and religious, more than a few Bishops, and a few Cardinals departing from the one true Church by rejecting the holy Roman Pontiff and his teachings. The vast majority of persons who now call themselves Catholic will formally reject Catholicism and leave the Church. Some will become Protestant. Some will attempt to set up a competing Church, which they will claim is the "true" Church. Most will simply depart from Christianity altogether (hence the term "apostasy").

But as I've said above, the Warning initiates the tribulation; it is the threshold event, since the sufferings of the tribulation, as the Seven Seals, do not begin until after the Warning, Consolation, and Miracle. So the great apostasy cannot occur before the Warning. At the time of the Warning, most Catholics will remain as Catholics. Once the severe afflictions of the tribulation begin, and as they unfold and worsen, the faith of many will be shaken, and most will depart from the Church.

What I expect to happen, though, is a set of preparatory events prior to the Warning. These events prepare for the tribulation. Concerning the great apostasy, I believe the preparatory event is a conflict between conservative Catholics, especially traditionalists, and Pope Francis. Many are already criticizing the holy Pontiff, undermining his teachings, rejecting his personal opinions even on matters of religion, and presenting their own pious opinions as if these were dogma. Some conservatives are openly speaking about the possibility of a pope falling into heresy -- which as I have explained at length in my other writings, can never occur. They are ready to leave the Church if Pope Francis will only teach any truth from Divine Revelation contrary to their own limited understanding, misunderstanding, false assumptions, erroneous conclusions, and arrogant claims. For they speak as if their view of Catholicism could never err; it is as if they were infallible.

I believe that Pope Francis, in 2015, will teach one or more truths from Divine Revelation that are contrary to the ideas of many conservatives and traditionalists. And they will respond by accusing the Pope of heresy; in this way, they will depart from the one true Church, falling into schism and heresy themselves.

Which truths will Pope Francis faithfully teach, in the year 2015, that will initiate this reaction, this starting point for the great apostasy? My understanding is that he will teach that the Church has the authority to ordain women to the diaconate, and he will plan for the start of women's ordination as deaconesses in January of 2016.

You can find my lengthy explanation on this topic in my other theology writings. For now, I will simply explain that the current teaching of the Magisterium on women's ordination is often misunderstood. The Church does not teach that "women cannot be ordained", but rather that Christ did not give His Church the authority to ordain women to the priesthood. The teaching specifies, and is limited to, the exclusion of women from priestly ordination. The current teaching of the Magisterium is this infallible doctrine:

> "Wherefore, in order that all doubt may be removed regarding a matter of great importance, a matter which pertains to the Church's divine constitution itself, in virtue of my ministry of confirming the brethren (cf. Lk 22:32) I declare that the Church has no authority whatsoever to confer priestly ordination on women and that this judgment is to be definitively held by all the Church's faithful." (Ordinatio Sacerdotalis 4).

I say that this teaching falls under Papal Infallibility. But the more common opinion is that it falls under the infallibility of the ordinary and universal Magisterium. In any case, the teaching is infallible. But notice the form of this teaching. It does not say "women can never be ordained". It specifies priestly ordination, which leaves ordination to the diaconate as an open question.

My considered theological opinion is that the Church possesses the authority to ordain women to the diaconate. I believe that Pope Francis will teach this doctrine in 2015, and will plan for the start of women's ordination to the diaconate in 2016. However, as a believing and practicing Roman Catholic, I will certainly adhere to whatever the Magisterium decides on this question. I only tell you my opinion on this particular point because I think that this controversy is one that initiates the great apostasy.

Another likely doctrinal controversy, during the reign of Pope Francis, is on the topic of salvation theology. My own theological opinion, based on my research into magisterial teachings on the subject, is that non-Catholic Christians can be saved without converting to Catholicism, non-Christian believers can be saved without converting to Christianity, and unbelievers (atheists, agnostics) can be saved without converting to belief in God. How can this be?

Refusal to convert is objectively a grave sin. But a person might be in good conscience, mistakenly thinking that God does not exist, or mistakenly thinking that Christianity or Catholicism is not the truest form of religion. Each human person is judged by his or her conscience. A person can enter the state of grace by an implicit baptism of desire, and a person can repent from actual mortal sin by implicit perfect contrition. So the path of salvation is accessible to all human persons. But the further one gets from Catholic Christian belief and practice, the more difficult the path to Heaven becomes.

Concerning the conflict between Pope Francis and conservatives or traditionalists, if the Pope teaches (what I understand to be true) that people can be saved apart from formal membership in the Church, apart from Christianity or even belief in God, I'm certain that most traditionalists and many conservatives will reject his teaching and depart from the one true Church. Ironically, they will depart from the Church while saying that one can only be saved by the Church.

Now on the one hand, it is true that "there is no salvation apart from the Church". But the Church includes all persons who are in a state of grace, and a person can be in a state of grace without being a Catholic, or a Christian, or even a believer. For the true selfless love of neighbor always includes, at least implicitly, the love of God. Some members of the Church are not Christian, and some do not believe in God. Theirs is a mystical membership.

Perhaps the reader disagrees with my understanding of salvation theology. Until the Magisterium settles the matter definitively, you are free to believe any theological opinion compatible with past teachings. But many conservative Catholics are unaware that Pope Saint John Paul II taught a liberal view of salvation theology in his encyclical Redemptoris Missio.

> "The universality of salvation means that it is granted not only to those who explicitly believe in Christ and have entered the Church. Since salvation is offered to all, it must be made concretely available to all."[6]

> "However, as I wrote in the Encyclical Redemptoris Missio, the gift of salvation cannot be limited 'to those who explicitly believe in Christ and have entered the Church. Since salvation is offered to all, it must be made concretely available to all.' "[7]

See my book *Forgiveness and Salvation for Everyone*, for more on this topic. What I would like the reader to understand is that, if Pope Francis teaches a liberal view of salvation theology, many conservatives and most traditionalists will be likely to reject him and his teaching. But they are in no way justified in that rejection.

The correct answer to each question on faith and morals is not necessarily the conservative answer. Jesus did not teach His disciples to be conservatives or liberals. Some of His teachings might be considered liberal, some moderate, some conservative. But at the present time, many conservative Catholics reject all that seems liberal, and many liberal Catholics reject all that seems conservative.

I expect that, in 2015, Pope Francis will teach both of the above controversial doctrines: on the diaconate and on salvation. Perhaps he will surprise us with further teachings, truths found in Divine Revelation, newly clarified under his reign. I welcome teaching and correction from each successive Pope. But I know that the vast majority of Catholics only want teachers who tell them what they already think is true. And they don't accept correction from anyone.

Pope Francis may also upset conservatives with some of his decisions on discipline. He may change Canon Law to make it easier for the divorced and remarried to receive Communion. He may change Canon Law to permit married men to become Catholic priests, as a response to the shortage of priests in some nations. He may loosen the rules for the form of the Mass, allowing the priest celebrating Mass to make changes to the form. Each of these points is largely a matter of discipline, not doctrine. But some conservatives and many traditionalists speak as if they decide what is and is not proper discipline. They condemn any Papal decisions contrary to their own thinking. They lack humility and obedience.

When Pope Francis teaches truths contrary to the ideas prevalent among conservatives, many will depart from the Church. But most Catholics will remain Catholic, in the year 2015. Later, as women begin to be ordained as deacons in 2016, and perhaps as the teaching on salvation theology is explained to the Church, more conservatives will depart. This is only stage one of the great apostasy. It is the first wave of departures from the Church.

A second wave of departures occurs after the Warning. Many of those Catholics who did not repent of their grave sins in response to the Warning will leave the Church. They will not want to be reminded of their unrepentant sins by continuing to be Catholic. Many will turn away from all religion as a result.

The reign of Pope Francis will be brief, and his successor will be very conservative. My understanding, as an idea in speculative eschatology, is that Cardinal Arinze will become the next Pope as Pope Pius XIII (Pious the 13th). But whoever is elected Pope, he will be very conservative. Yet he will not reject or contradict the controversial teachings of Pope Francis. So those traditionalists and conservatives who departed under Pope Francis will remain separated from the Church.

Then this next conservative Pope will teach doctrines offensive to liberal Catholics. He will restrict Communion and the other Sacraments to those who actually believe and practice the Catholic faith. He will reject many of the ideas popular in sinful secular society and among liberal Catholics. Then the third wave of departures from the Church will occur, completing the great apostasy. At that time, a vast number of liberal and moderate Catholics will depart from the Church.

The sufferings of the tribulation also play a role in the great apostasy. It is more difficult to deal with a conflict, internal or external, in matters of faith, when you are suffering and in fear of death. Some who are weak in faith will despair of the mercy of God, leading them to fall away from Christianity altogether. Many liberal Catholics just ignore any teaching or rule of the Church with which they disagree. But as the sufferings of the tribulation weigh upon them, one difficulty after another, and secular society becomes more hateful toward Catholicism, they will depart from the Church.

So the great apostasy begins in 2015, prior to the Warning on Good Friday of 2016. But the main portion of the apostasy does not unfold until after the Warning and Miracle have occurred and the sufferings of the tribulation have begun in earnest.

Before the Warning: a Prelude to War

The first affliction of the tribulation is the first Seal in the Book of Revelation, also called the Apocalypse of John.

[Revelation 6]
{6:1} And I saw that the Lamb had opened one of the seven seals. And I heard one of the four living creatures saying, in a voice like thunder: "Draw near and see."
{6:2} And I saw, and behold, a white horse. And he who was sitting upon it was holding a bow, and a crown was given to him, and he went forth conquering, so that he might prevail.

My interpretation is that this event of the first Seal, which is also termed the first horseman of the apocalypse, is World War 3. This war is a conflict between nations led by Muslim extremists and the West, primarily Europe and the United States. In my opinion, World War 3 will begin soon after the Warning and Miracle, all in 2016. But what we are discussing now is events prior to the Warning, specifically events that prepare for World War 3.

We can easily see the preparations for this war in the world today. The Arab/Muslim nations of the Middle East and northern Africa have increasingly come under the influence of extremists. The old order of dictators, who were not very religious, controlling those Muslim nations is passing away. In its place, Muslim extremists are rising to power. The Arab Spring was thought to bring democracy to that region of the world. Instead, it removed evil dictators, but also cleared the way for Muslim extremists to rise to power.

The Islamic State, also called ISIS or ISIL, is the extremist group currently rising to power in Iraq and Syria. I expect that they will continue to be successful in conquering more territory, and that they will gain control of Iraq. Iran and Iraq and the other Muslim nations of that region will eventually all be controlled by extremists. They will band together, under the dual leadership of Iran and Iraq (apparently with Iraq controlled by ISIL).

The Book of Daniel, in my interpretation, describes World War 3 as initiated by Persia and Media (Daniel 8). Persian is an ancient kingdom located in present-day Iran. Media is an ancient kingdom based in present-day Iraq, but extending into Syria and other regions of the Middle East. So my interpretation is that Iran and Iraq will lead the other Muslim nations of that region into war with the West.

Prior to the Warning, I expect the progress toward this war to continue. This implies that ISIL will continue to gain power and territory, and will gain control of Iraq. ISIL will also gain power by allying with other extremists. And as I understand the text of Daniel, once ISIL controls Iraq, they will make an alliance with Iran. For it is these two nations that lead the other Muslim nations in World War 3 against the West.

This conclusion also suggests that Iran will complete its long quest to obtain nuclear weapons. For they cannot hope to defeat Europe without nuclear weapons. See my book *On World War 3 and World War 4* for the details. In summary, Iran has been enriching uranium and otherwise working toward the goal of making its own nuclear weapons. At this point in time, in November of 2014, they are close. It may be that they have a covert facility, unknown to the West, which is already producing weapon-grade uranium for several nuclear weapons.

Iran is one of the nations that attacks the West in World War 3.

[Daniel 8]
{8:1} In the third year of the reign of Belshazzar the king, a vision appeared to me. After that which I had seen in the beginning, I, Daniel,

25

{8:2} saw in my vision, that I was in the capital city of Susa, which is in the region of Elam [*a region in Iran*], yet I saw in the vision that I was over the gate of Ulai.

{8:3} And I lifted up my eyes and saw, and behold, a single ram stood before the marsh, having two high horns, and one was higher than the other and growing higher still.

{8:4} After this, I saw the ram brandishing his horns against the West, and against the North, and against the Meridian, and all the beasts could not withstand him, nor be freed from his hand, and he did according to his own will, and he became great.

...

{8:19} And he said to me, "I will reveal to you what the future things are in the earlier tribulation, for the time has its end.

{8:20} The ram, which you saw to have horns, is the king of the Medes and Persians.

Iran is Persia. Sacred Scripture prophecies that Iran and the other nations in that region, represented by the Medes, will attack to the West (the U.S.) and to the North (Europe), and "against the Meridian", i.e. southward toward the equator, in Africa. The fact that Iran is close to obtaining nuclear weapons only strengths the interpretation that Iran is the nation that the Book of Daniel predicted would initiate the tribulation by attacks on the West.

The first part of the tribulation includes a sequence of events, described in the Book of Revelation under the figures of the first six Seals, and the first six Trumpets of the seventh Seal (Rev 5:1 to 9:21). These events occur in the order described in the Bible, over a certain period of time, ending with the Three Days of Darkness in late March of 2040 A.D. I believe that the secrets of Medjugorje, and to some extent the secrets of Garabandal, describe the events of the first part of the tribulation. The reason that there has been such an increase in the number of true private revelations in recent decades is to prepare the faithful for the tribulation, whose start is marked by three extraordinary events: the Warning, the Consolation, the Miracle. But because the world is so sinful, God also permits false private revelations (which are generally from fallen angels).

The tribulation begins with the first horseman of the apocalypse:

[Revelation 6]
{6:1} And I saw that the Lamb had opened one of the seven seals. And I heard one of the four living creatures saying, in a voice like thunder: "Draw near and see."
{6:2} And I saw, and behold, a white horse. And he who was sitting upon it was holding a bow, and a crown was given to him, and he went forth conquering, so that he might prevail.

This war is the same as the war described by Daniel, in which the Arab/Muslim nations of the Middle East and northern Africa, led by Iran and Iraq, attack the West. And war is fast approaching. Once Iran obtains nuclear weapons, World War 3 will be imminent. For the Iranian regime adheres to a radical set of ideas in Muslim eschatology, including the idea that it is Iran's duty to initiate (the Islamic extremist version of) the end times by making war against the West.

As I have been saying for many years in my books of Catholic eschatology, World War 3 begins with a nuclear attack on New York City. Iran sends a nuclear bomb to New York, most probably by ship, and explodes it in the city, perhaps near the United Nations buildings. This occurs not many weeks after the Miracle, in the same year: 2016. This horrific unprovoked attack marks the start of World War 3 and of the tribulation.

The Warning, and another event I term "the Consolation", and finally the Miracle all prepare the human person -- in soul, spirit, body -- for the events of the tribulation. The Warning benefits the soul by showing us our sins, and offering the gift of repentance from sin. The Consolation benefits the spirit by consoling those who are still grieving over their sins after the Warning. The Miracle heals the body of innumerable persons (but not all) throughout the world, and also heals the soul by strengthening faith. These three blessings prepare us for the tribulation.

The first four events of the tribulation are the same as the first four Seals in the Book of Revelation. These are the 'four horsemen' of the Apocalypse:

(1) World War 3,
(2) worldwide severe civil violence and disorder,
(3) a famine especially in wealthy nations,
(4) death from a variety of different causes (Rev 6:1-6:8).

And these events of the four horsemen must occur in the 2010's and no later, because time is needed in the 2020's and 2030's for all the subsequent events: the occupation of Europe after the war, the brief but severe war (World War 4) of the long-prophesied great Catholic monarch to free Europe from the occupation, and a subsequent severe set of sufferings which complete the Seven Seals, except for the seventh trumpet of the seventh seal, which occurs during the second part of the tribulation (hundreds of years later).

So the start of the tribulation must occur very soon after the Warning, Consolation, and Miracle occur. The Warning is certainly a warning to fallen sinners to repent. But it occurs before the start of the tribulation, so as to warn us to repent in preparation for that severe set of afflictions. It is a warning to our souls, that we must place spiritual goods above temporal goods, at all times, but especially during the difficulties of the tribulation, if we are to survive without losing our salvation. Otherwise, we may die in our sins.

[John]
{8:21} Therefore, Jesus again spoke to them: "I am going, and you shall seek me. And you will die in your sin. Where I am going, you are not able to go."
{8:22} And so the Jews said, "Is he going to kill himself, for he said: 'Where I am going, you are not able to go?' "
{8:23} And he said to them: "You are from below. I am from above. You are of this world. I am not of this world.

{8:24} Therefore, I said to you, that you will die in your sins. For if you will not believe that I am, you will die in your sin."
{8:25} And so they said to him, "Who are you?" Jesus said to them: "The Beginning, who is also speaking to you.

How does the Warning relate to the first affliction of the tribulation, World War 3? My understanding is that, when the Warning occurs, many sinful persons will reject the call to repentance; they will react with fear, rather than sorrow for sin. And in those nations where Islamic extremists have much support, some persons will repent, but many will not. Instead, the extremists, having been stricken by God in their consciences, will make a desperate grab for power. For they will fear that sorrow for sin will take away their power, which is based on sinful violence and oppression and false religious teachings.

Thus, the Warning initiates the consolidation of power of the extremists over the Arab/Muslim nations of the Middle East and northern Africa. There will be coups and uprisings in those nations not yet controlled by extremists at the time of the Warning. And they will all quickly band together, out of fear, under the leadership of Iran and Iraq.

Then, when the Miracle occurs, healing many persons throughout the world, and leaving permanent miraculous signs at places of true private revelation in the Catholic Christian religion, the Islamic extremists will fear a total loss of power, due to the rise of influence of Catholic Christianity in response to the Miracle. Their fear and desperation will reach new heights, and they will sweep away the last obstacles to their control over the Arab/Muslim nations of the Middle East and northern Africa. They will also rush into World War 3, much sooner than they might otherwise have done, due to their fearful sinful response to the Warning and the Miracle.

After the Warning, as a result of the acceptance of the gift of repentance by many persons, the world will become somewhat less sinful. After the Miracle, as a result of the Permanent Signs, many unbelievers will convert, so that the world again will become somewhat less sinful. But the tribulation will continue to unfold, because many persons will remain unrepentant, and many will relapse into their former sins. Thus, there will be a continuing spiritual conflict, during the tribulation, between the repentant and the unrepentant.

Joey Lomangino

At Garabandal the Virgin Mary said that the Miracle will cure a blind man, named Joey Lomangino, so that he will see. But in 2014, Joey died in his elder years, having been born about 1930.[8] There has been must discussion online among adherents of Garabandal as to what this might mean.

Some have suggested that Joey's death means that the prophecies of Garabandal are false. I disagree. True private revelation often requires a proper interpretation in order for its truths to be known. And the Blessed Virgin Mary does not always speak plainly in the messages of private revelation, as she does not want to eclipse the teaching authority of the Church and the teachings of Scripture. So when she speaks about the future, her words are veiled and may require some interpretation.

I have spent many years studying claimed private revelations, writing articles (available on my website CatholicPlanet.com) with explanations as to why one is false and another is true. What I have learned is that the false private revelations contain many doctrinal errors, and they exalt the claimed visionary. Then, by comparison, the true private revelations are consistent with Church teaching, yet some interpretation is required, and some misunderstanding is possible. I find the private revelation at Garabandal to be true and worthy of the confidence of faithful Catholics. And the same is true for Medjugorje.

So what is the explanation as to why Joey died, when so many were expecting him to be healed miraculously at the Miracle of Garabandal? I am not certain. Some have suggested that his body will be discovered to be incorrupt and to have new eyes after the Miracle occurs. Others have suggested he might be resurrected -- but I must interject that this is not possible prior to the Resurrection described in Sacred Scripture (and that time is of the distant future). A more likely suggestion is that the Blessed Virgin Mary simply meant that he would see the Miracle and the many healings throughout the world (including the blind seeing) from his place in Heaven.

In any case, the death of Joey has not shaken my faith in the messages of Garabandal, nor in the predictions that the Warning and the Miracle will occur.

Before the Warning: Politics and Religion

The Warning will occur when things are at their worst, as the visionaries of Garabandal have said. Thus, the world will be very sinful at the time of the Warning. As every faithful Catholic knows, the world has increased in sinfulness in recent decades. And as each year passes, things seem to get worse. Sinful secular society has become exceedingly immoral.

Even in nations where most persons are nominally Christian, the Christian faith is rejected and devout believers are persecuted. The reason for this paradox is that most Christians, including Catholics and Protestants, have essentially fallen away from the true Faith. They have become non-practicing or minimally-practicing Christians. And most of those Catholics who attend Mass regularly do not believe all that the Church teaches. They believe whatever they like. They adopt whatever ideas are prevalent in sinful secular society at the time, in contradiction to Catholic teaching. And they do not see the Pope as their teacher. Truly, the foundation for the great apostasy had been laid.

It is well-known that politicians respond well to the majority opinion among their constituents. Otherwise, they would not be elected or re-elected. So when a nation becomes ever more sinful, and when that nation accepts ideas contrary to truth on matters of

' morals, the politicians adopt the same ideas. But worse ‚ they tend to incorporate those harmful ideas into law and policy. And this makes it more difficult for faithful Catholic Christians to live a holy life in such a nation.

Fortunately, the Warning will have a good effect on politics and society. So very many persons will repent of their sins that politicians -- repentant or not -- will have to change law and policy to accommodate the faithful. This will enrage unrepentant sinners. But they will fail, in the short term, to reassert their dominance over secular society.

Spiritual Communism

The visionaries were informed at Garabandal that communism would be widespread at the time that the Warning occurs. But this information came to them from the Virgin Mary in Heaven. Mary speaks to us from Heaven in a heavenly manner, giving spiritual values their proper place above temporal values. Therefore, I would interpret her words from a spiritual point of view. It is not political communism that will be widespread at the time of the Warning, but spiritual communism.

Spiritual communism is a kind of false equality which denies different roles for men and women, denies different roles for ordained and non-ordained persons, denies different roles for deacons versus priests versus bishops, denies that there are absolute truths (all opinions are said to be equal or are treated as if equal), denies different roles based on age, denies different roles based on the will of God for each person. Instead, spiritual communism promotes the idea that anyone can take any role, according to whatever pleases them, and that all opinions are of equal value. This idea denigrates the distinctions between human persons and denigrates the will of God based on those distinctions. It denies the fittingness of roles given to persons based on differences in gender, age, state of life, and ability. It also gives incorrect or false opinions the same standing as truth. It is a false equality, a false claim of fairness. This is spiritual communism. And it is already widespread.

Also, if we examine the state of the world today, it is clear to many persons that the tribulation is imminent. And yet political communism is not poised to immerse the world in a major war, such as would fit the Bible's description of the first horseman (and first seal) of the apocalypse. Instead, radical Islam is threatening the world, the Christians nations of the West, and the nation of Israel. Many people do not realize that Nazi terrorism was one of the preludes to World War 2. Similarly, terrorism by Muslim extremists is a prelude to World War 3.

So it is not political communism that threatens the world today. Mary was not saying that political communism would be widespread at the time of the Warning, but rather spiritual communism. She was warning us about that spiritual communism, which is already widespread in secular society, and also widespread among many members of the Church on earth.

In my view, the wars that occur during the first part of the tribulation are not related to political communism. At Garabandal, when the Virgin Mary was asked about the fears at that time (in the early 1960's) of a world war between the superpowers (U.S., Soviet Union, China), she answered that there would be no such world war. A world war based on the conflict between communism and democracy does not occur during the first part of the tribulation. Instead, the two major wars of that time are based on the conflict between Christianity and extremist Islam, between Western culture and Arab/Muslim culture.

I believe that the Warning will occur just before the start of the tribulation, for sin and spiritual communism are already widespread. The Warning, Consolation, and Miracle refresh and strengthen the souls of the faithful, to prepare them for the afflictions of the tribulation. But the many souls who refuse to repent, or who soon relapse into old sins, will be filled with fear and desperation in response to these three great blessings.

Then the start of the tribulation increases the fear and desperation of unrepentant sinners. But instead of turning to God and to His Church for guidance, they increase their own sinfulness. This will include an increase in their insistence on the false equality called spiritual communism, and an attempt to blame religion for the sufferings of the tribulation.

Many persons will break away from the Catholic Church, and even try to form their own false church, one that incorporates this false equality by approving of women priests, and by denigrating the role of the Bishops and priests over the laity. This event is part of the great apostasy; it is partly caused by spiritual communism among Catholics. They refuse to acknowledge the Pope and the Magisterium of the Church as their teacher. For they think that all ideas and opinions are of equal value, and that their own decisions on matters of faith and morals should be considered equal to the definitive teachings of the Church.

The visionaries of Garabandal, when speaking of spiritual communism, described both the time leading up to the Warning and the time following the Warning, in the early years of the tribulation:

> Mari Loli: "It would look like the communists have taken over the whole world and it would be very hard to practice the religion, for priests to say Mass or for the people to open the doors of the churches."[9]

In my interpretation, this refers to spiritual communism, not political communism. This affliction of the spread of spiritual communism begins prior to the Warning, in fact it is already widespread in the world. But as the great apostasy unfolds, the effects on the Church will worsen. The great apostasy begins before the Warning, and worsens afterward. Only after the tribulation begins will it be so bad as to make it difficult for priests to say Mass or for a church to remain open.

The first wave of departures from the Church, as part of the great apostasy occurs prior to the Warning. Then many conservatives will depart from the Church, in reaction to the true teachings of Pope Francis (in 2015). These departures will cause confusion within many of the more conservative parishes, but few parishes will shut down or join the schism. Most Catholics and most parishes will not depart from the Church at that time.

When the Warning occurs, a second wave of Catholics will depart from the Church. Those Catholics who refuse to repent of their sins in response to the Warning will react by departing from the Church. To continue as members of the Church without repenting will be too difficult for them, as they will correctly understand that the Church rebukes sinners for their unrepentant sins.

The Warning certainly brings many Catholics to a sincere and full repentance. Those Catholics who repent include already faithful Catholics, minimally practicing Catholics, practicing Catholics who had been unrepentant from certain sins, and even many non-practicing Catholics. So one reaction to the Warning will be a renewal of faith in Catholicism. But not all Catholics will accept the offer to repent. And many who refuse to repent will depart from the Church, resulting in this second wave of departures in the great apostasy.

Finally, after the Warning and Miracle, the afflictions of the tribulation begin. Then the next conservative Pope (the Pope after Pope Francis) will offend liberal Catholics by teaching the truth. The combination of severe afflictions of the tribulation and a rebuke of sin by the Pope will result in a third wave of Catholics leaving the Church, completing the great apostasy.

The Catholic faith will be hard to practice because so many priests and laypersons will have left the Faith. Many parishes will have no priest and few parishioners, and so they will be forced to close. Most dioceses will not have enough money to continue their usual operations, due to a vast decrease in Mass attendance; they will have to lay off staff and cut back on services. In some churches, the priest and the parishioners will have broken away from the Catholic Church entirely. In some dioceses, the bishop himself will break away from the Church. As a result, it will be hard for the remaining priests to say Mass, and hard for the remaining faithful to practice the faith.

> Jacinta: "The Virgin said that the Warning would come when conditions were at their worst. It wouldn't be just the persecution either because many people will no longer be practicing their religion."[10]

The Garabandal visionary named Jacinta explicitly said that many persons will have stopped practicing their religion. I would interpret this to mean that the departures from the Church begin before the Warning, but also continue afterward. For this phrasing is an accurate description of the great apostasy.

Jacinta also mentioned that there would be persecution of Catholics. We already see some persecution of Catholics by sinful secular society due to the disparity between Catholic teaching and the ideas of society on how people should live and act. This conflict will increase as the tribulation unfolds, making it difficult for the weak in faith to persevere in the Faith.

Eventually, as the tribulation continues to afflict the world and the Church continues to teach and to console the world, many of those Catholics who departed from the Church will return. Then, as they return, many Protestants -- who benefited from the Warning, Consolation, and Miracle in 2016 -- will seek to join the Catholic Church. The early 2020's (from mid-2020 to late 2023) will see a restructuring of the one Church to include Protestants, Orthodox, and Catholics in one Roman Catholic Church.

This return of the Protestants to the Church was foretold by Jesus in the parable of the Prodigal Son. But recall that the elder son refused to join the celebration, and chose to remain outside the family. The elder son represents those Catholic traditionalists who reject the unification of all Christians in one Catholic Church. So they will remain outside the Church, until they repent. See Luke chapter 15.

Time of Day

The Warning of Garabandal must occur on a Good Friday because the meaning of this event is closely tied to the Crucifixion of Christ on the Cross. All the grace that anyone ever receives to repent from sin and be forgiven is dispensed from the Cross by Jesus Christ. Therefore, I conclude that the Warning will occur on Good Friday, at the same time when the Crucifixion occurred.

In my book, *Important Dates in the Lives of Jesus and Mary*, I determined that Jesus died on April 7th, 19 A.D. about the ninth hour of the day (by the ancient method of marking the hours used by the Jews) in Jerusalem. This time corresponds to between 2:50 and 2:51 p.m. Israel Standard Time. The ninth hour of the day is the midpoint between solar noon and sunset. The exact time of this midpoint depends on the length of daylight for that particular day of the year.

On Good Friday of 2016, which is March 25th, many nations will be keeping track of the hours using daylight savings time, which moves the time ahead one hour from standard time. However, Israel does not switch to Daylight Savings Time (called 'Israel Summer Time') in 2016, until April 1st. In any case, 2:51 p.m. Israel Standard Time would correspond to 8:51 a.m. Eastern Daylight Time in the United States on March 25th of 2016. This same time can be expressed in Coordinated Universal Time (UTC), which ignores daylight savings time, as 12:51 UTC.

The Warning occurs everywhere in the world at the same moment, that is, simultaneously. So the time on the clock will be different depending on the time zone in each area of the world.

I believe that the Warning will occur at the same time as the Crucifixion, and that the Crucifixion occurred at about 2:51 p.m. Israel Standard Time. If I am correct on these two points, then the

Warning will begin about 8:51 a.m. Eastern Daylight Time (12:51 UTC). In any case, the day and time of the Warning is based on the day and time of the Crucifixion.

The Warning: What will happen?

It begins with an event in the sky. This event is not natural, but supernatural (or preternatural, i.e. caused by angels). This event is not the Warning itself. This event has no effect on nature or on the planet. This event is not a comet, nor an asteroid, nor any other natural event. The purpose of this event is to get everyone's attention, and to awaken anyone who is sleeping. It is very brief, even momentary. This event is NOT the appearance in the sky of a cross or crucifix or other Christian religious image.

It has been said by Conchita, one of the visionaries of Garabandal, that this event begins with the letter 'A'.[11] I believe that the 'A' stands for Angel, because this is not a natural event, and because God often makes use of His Angels to herald His Divine Acts. (Technically, the action of angels is called preternatural, not supernatural.)

Just before the actual event of the Warning, God sends a holy Angel (or multiple holy Angels) to cause a loud sound and a bright light in the sky. The sound will be heard everywhere on earth. The light will be seen everywhere on earth. The purpose is merely to get everyone's attention, so that they awaken, if asleep, so that they pay attention to the Warning. Then the actual event of the Warning occurs.

Everything will stop during the brief time needed for the Warning (minutes, not hours). Electronics and vehicles will not function, except in cases of necessity. People who are asleep will be awakened for this event.

The Warning itself is entirely supernatural. Each person will find themselves alone in their mind and heart with their conscience. God will touch each person's soul. God will enlighten each person's conscience in a way which is fitting to the uniqueness of each individual, within the limits of each person's knowledge and experiences. People will understand the sins and the negative consequences of their sins, but only in so far as any sin remains on the conscience and unforgiven. Catholics who have recently made a good confession will have the least sins on their conscience.

The Warning illuminates the conscience, but does not provide any type of Divine Revelation. The knowledge that is obtained by the Warning about each person's own sins is essentially the same type of knowledge that could have been obtained by a very thorough examination of conscience. So this event does not compete with Sacred Tradition, Sacred Scripture, or the Magisterium as sources of truth on faith or morals.

In an interview, Conchita gave a succinct and accurate description of this event:

> "the Warning will be like a revelation of our sins -- and it will be seen and experienced equally by believers and non-believers and people of any religion whatsoever.... The Warning will be a correction of the conscience of the world."[12]

Every single human person on earth without exception will experience the Warning. Every single human person on earth will be offered grace and mercy directly from God. Even prenatals in the womb will be touched by God; though they have no personal sins to be brought to mind, they will be given blessings of grace to prepare them for the great difficulties of the world into which they will be born, especially the gift of God's grace to strengthen them against sin (but they will not be sinless).

For most persons, those who are old enough to understand right from wrong, the Warning will take the form of an awakening of the conscience, making that person aware of his current unrepentant sins and tendency toward sin. God will offer all sinners the gift of repentance and conversion from these sins, as well as grace and mercy more generally.

For those who are holy and have few sins, and for those who have thoroughly repented from their sins and been forgiven, the experience will be different. For them, their sorrow will be at the sufferings of Jesus Christ on the Cross for the sins of mankind, much more than over their own sins. They will join with Jesus Christ in His loving sorrow for the sinfulness of the world.

Those who are evil will no longer be able to hide behind excuses for their sins. They will no longer be able to half-deceive themselves. They will know full well that what they have done is evil. People often lie to themselves, telling themselves that what they are doing is right, when they know in their heart of hearts that it is wrong. But at the Warning, these lies will be exposed. There will be no place to hide from the truths of one's conscience at the time of the Warning.

Some great sinners will repent greatly. But many great sinners will continue in their evil deeds, with a much clearer realization that they have chosen evil over good. By rejecting this gift of repentance, and by deliberately choosing to continue sinning, despite a very full knowledge that what they are choosing is evil, they will commit actual mortal sins and will become much more thoroughly evil themselves. The fallen angels will concentrate their efforts on such persons, over whom they will have greater influence than before.

Actual Mortal Sin

Be Advised: anyone who rejects the gift of repentance on the Day of the Warning is necessarily committing an actual mortal sin, because the Warning carries with it a clarity of heart and mind to such a full extent that only by an act of full deliberation and full knowledge can one reject this extraordinary call from God to repentance from sin. The call to repent from sin on this day is grave matter; therefore, deliberately and knowingly rejecting it is an actual mortal sin.

The Warning: What it is not

Be Advised: there are numerous false visionaries and other persons who are promoting false ideas about the Warning! Some of these visionaries have plagiarized my work in eschatology, claiming it as their own and also distorting some truths into falsehoods. Do not believe a visionary merely because he or she spoke about the Warning before it happened. Some of these persons are also plagiarizing dates and times from my work, as if they themselves had perceived the timing of these events.

The Warning has its limits. It will not reveal all knowledge about religion or about morals. It will not make all non-Catholic Christians realize that Catholicism is the truest form of Christianity. It will not make all non-Christians realize that Christianity is the truest form of religion.

It will not give the very young the understanding of adults. It will not speak to each person beyond the limits of their own knowledge, understanding, and experiences. It will not provide people with a complete understanding of right and wrong. It will not provide people with a complete understanding of their entire life. It will not show each person their entire life. It will not show each person the good things that they have done in their life. It is restrained by the limits inherent to each person's mind and heart and life. Each person will NOT see their soul as God sees it.

The Warning is NOT a mini-judgment, comparable to the particular judgment of the soul before God, an event which occurs immediately after death. The Warning provides an understanding of the sins on one's conscience only, not a review of all sins in life, not a review of all the good and bad that one has done in life.

Since the Warning only affects the sins on one's conscience, a person will NOT be corrected during the Warning for sinful acts committed with a sincere but mistaken conscience. After the Warning, some persons will say that they must be correct in continuing their past behavior, since the Warning did not show it to them as a sin. But that is not true. If their past behavior were objectively a sin, even a grave sin, but were committed with a sincere by mistaken conscience, the Warning will not correct that sin. The Warning is a great blessing, but it is not so great and full as to replace Sacred Tradition, Sacred Scripture, the Magisterium, and the Church. That is why the Warning has its limits.

The Warning is not the end of the world. The Warning is not an immediate precursor to the end of the world, nor does it herald the Return of Jesus Christ. The end of the world is not for this generation, nor for the next, nor for the next, nor until centuries afterward. The Antichrist is not in the world today, and he will not be born for several centuries. Do not believe or follow any visionary who claims that Jesus returns for this generation, or that the Antichrist is in the world today, or any similar claim.

The end times in Catholic eschatology do not refer to the immediate end of the world, but to a long period of time leading up to the Return of Christ. So the beginning of the end times is not to be understood as the end of the world. But in my understanding the tribulation is divided into two parts, and those parts are a few centuries apart. So even after the tribulation begins and after the Warning and Miracle occur, the Return of Christ will still be in the distant future.

The Warning is NOT the first Seal of the Book of Revelation, nor is it the first of the four horsemen of the apocalypse. The first Seal is a great war: World War 3 (Rev 6:1-2).

The Warning: Individual Reactions

All human souls will be touched by God in some manner pertaining to sin and grace. Many people will become holier and less sinful. Many people will repent. Many will continue in this repentance, reforming their lives and seeking God. Many others will quickly relapse, falling back into sin, perhaps even into worse sins. Some will reject the Warning so thoroughly that they will become very much more sinful than ever before.

Many Catholics, after the Warning, will anxiously seek a better understanding of Catholic teaching, especially on ethics. Most Catholics today are poorly taught; they know very little about the Church's teaching on faith and morals. See my book *The Catechism of Catholic Ethics: a work of Roman Catholic moral theology* for a comprehensive explanation of Catholic teaching on morality.

Many false teachers will rise up after the Warning, in an attempt to convince others of their false ideas about faith and morals. Be cautious whom you accept as a teacher. There will be much controversy and confusion after the Warning as to which explanation of ethics is correct.

Some will try to ignore or forget the Warning by indulgence in worldly pleasures. They will use alcohol, or drugs, or sex, or various type of entertainments to block out the truth of their sins. But this rejection of repentance from sin, at the time of the Warning, is itself a grave sin. God will hold this sin against them for the rest of their lives:

[Isaiah]
{22:12} And in that day, the Lord, the God of hosts, will call to weeping and mourning, to baldness and the wearing of sackcloth.
{22:13} But behold: gladness and rejoicing, the killing of calves and the slaughter of rams, the eating of meat and the drinking of wine: "Let us eat and drink, for tomorrow we will die."
{22:14} And the voice of the Lord of hosts was revealed in my ears: "Surely this iniquity will not be forgiven you, until you die," says the Lord, the God of hosts.

Some will be so afraid of having to face their own sins, mortal sins lived unrestrainedly for many years, that they will respond by taking their own lives. But suicide is not the answer. For after death, these persons will again have to face the sins of their lives and the consequences of their sins. Those who commit suicide will be punished by God, either in Purgatory or in Hell.

Many people will be struck by an overwhelming fear, confused about what has happened, not knowing to whom they should listen for an explanation of the event. Some persons will be so fearful that they will die of fright. The number dead from suicide and from fear will not be insignificant; it will be a small percentage, but a large number. This will represent a very sharp increase in the number of deaths from these causes at that time.

False Repentance

Beware of persons who attempt to feign repentance outwardly, when inwardly they have completely rejected God!!!

Some persons who experience the Warning will reject this merciful offer of repentance and forgiveness. But when they see many persons around them, sorrowing and repenting and seeking forgiveness, they will pretend to do the same. These false penitents will include some politicians, some news and media personalities, some celebrities, some members of the clergy and religious life, some lay persons with leadership roles, and some persons who might seem not to have any serious sins from which to refuse to repent. Very many of the mortal sins of humanity are hidden deep within the human person.

So beware of wolves in sheep's clothing!!! They will feign repentance in order to obtain or to maintain roles of leadership in society and in the Church, or for other reasons.

Group Reactions: The Church

The aftermath of the Warning will have profound effects on the Church, the world, families, and individual lives. It will change the current state of politics worldwide in a manner that is sudden and severe. It will change the course of the history of the human race and of the Church.

The Church will suddenly become holier, and will continue to increase in holiness. The transfiguration of Christ was a foreshadowing of this event, whereby the Church will be transfigured. But the transfiguration of the Church only begins with the Warning. It is not yet completed at this time. And so there will still be many problems in the Church for many more years. The completion of this transfiguration, at least for this generation, occurs many years later at the time of the Three Days of Darkness (March of 2040, which is 24 years after the Warning).

The Church on earth is comprised of sinners. Some of those sinners are very sinful and are harming the Church. The Warning will remove many sinful persons from the Church: some will die; some will reject the Church because they reject the gift of repentance offered by the Warning; some will be rejected by the faithful after the Warning because sincere repentance allows them to understand who is a true disciple of Christ, and who is not. So shall the Church be purified, to some extent, by this event. And the number who depart from the Church at this time will not be small; it is the second wave of the great apostasy.

In the days and weeks after the Warning, very many persons will flock to the Catholic Church for guidance and for the forgiveness of sins in the Sacrament of holy Confession. Priests will be overwhelmed with the number of repentant sinners who want to confess. (Prudent Catholics will go to confession frequently in the months and weeks prior to the Warning!) Even non-Catholics will want to go to Confession. The lines for confession will stretch out the doors of many churches. Only Catholics will know about this event in advance, and be able to explain its meaning, and be able to properly advise people as to how to be reconciled to God. Even Catholics who are not holy and not knowledgeable will be sought out by non-Catholics for whatever little guidance or knowledge they might be able to offer (cf. Zechariah 12:8).

But not every problem in the Church will be solved by the Warning. The Warning will not bestow all knowledge and understanding of right and wrong, even on holy persons. Christians will still disagree about beliefs and practices. Many repentant persons will slip back, some slowly, some quickly, into their old sins, or into worse sins. But this increase in holiness among the faithful will soon cause some barely-practicing Catholics and some non-practicing Catholics to fall away from the Church. For they will not be able to keep up with the quick advancement in holiness and in knowledge of the will of God that the Church will make, beginning at this time.

The Pope's Reaction

As I write these words in November of 2014, Pope Francis is the one true valid holy Pope, the head of the Church on earth. I believe that he will still be Pope when the Warning occurs on Good Friday of 2016. He is the Pope who initiates the great apostasy, prior to the Warning, by teaching truths from Divine Revelation. Yes, his teachings are truth. Some conservative Catholics, by a combination of pride and ignorance, have decided that certain erroneous ideas are dogma. They have misunderstood past teachings and drawn false conclusions. So when the Pope teaches that the Church has the authority to ordain women solely to the diaconate, they will reject him and depart in the first wave of the great apostasy. But the holy Pope Francis will not back down; he will permit women to become ordained deacons starting in January of 2016.

I believe that Pope Francis will also teach that non-Catholic Christians, non-Christian believers, and non-believers can each possibly be saved without converting to Catholicism, or Christianity, or belief in God. This truth is, in my understanding, entirely consistent with the teachings of his predecessors. But it is also a development of doctrine to some extent. See my book *Forgiveness and Salvation for Everyone* for a theological explanation as to how such persons might be saved without converting.

Pope Francis will be Pope at the time of the Warning. He will welcome the call to repentance, for he is a holy Pope and -- if you would believe me -- a future canonized Saint. He is the Pope mentioned in a mystical way in the passages of the Gospels which describe the Warning. For the Warning will result in a certain type of transfiguration of the Church.

[Mark 9]
{9:1} And after six days, Jesus took with him Peter, and James, and John; and he led them separately to a lofty mountain alone; and he was transfigured before them.
{9:2} And his vestments became radiant and exceedingly white like snow, with such a brilliance as no fuller on earth is able to achieve.
{9:3} And there appeared to them Elijah with Moses; and they were speaking with Jesus.
{9:4} And in response, Peter said to Jesus: "Master, it is good for us to be here. And so let us make three tabernacles, one for you, and one for Moses, and one for Elijah."
{9:5} For he did not know what he was saying. For they were overwhelmed by fear.
{9:6} And there was a cloud overshadowing them. And a voice came from the cloud, saying: "This is my most beloved Son. Listen to him."

The Pope who reigns at the time of the Warning is mentioned in Sacred Scripture in a hidden way. The transfiguration of Christ was a foreshadowing of the Warning. Peter said to Jesus, after His transfiguration: "Lord, it is good for us to be here. If you are willing, let us make three tabernacles here, one for you, one for Moses, and one for Elijah." (Mt 17:4). In this way, Peter foreshadowed this future Pope, who will respond to the Warning by suggesting that three places of worship (tabernacles) be established in Jerusalem: one for Christianity, one for Judaism, and one for Islam, that is, a Church, a Temple, and a Mosque. He will suggest that all three religions worship God together in peace, with the city of Jerusalem as an example in the sight of the whole world, an example of peace between religions.

The Gospel of Mark comments on Peter's words: "For he did not know what he was saying. For they were overwhelmed by fear." (Mk 9:5). The Pope suggests these three tabernacles because the world will be overwhelmed by fear in response to the Warning, and because they will seek answers to this event, each one in his own religion.

But the Pope's suggestion will not happen for many years. World War 3 will begin a few months after the Warning. Then, some years later, another even more devastating war, World War 4, will occur (in the 2030's). Not until after the first part of the tribulation (which ends in early 2040) will there be three places of worship in Jerusalem for the three religions (Christianity, Judaism, Islam). Not until then will there be a yearly celebration, at the same time of year, for worshipers from all three religions to worship together in peace in the city of peace (Zechariah 14:16-19).

There are already places of worship in Jerusalem, of course. But the three places that will be built will be three very important centers of worship. The Jews will be the first ones to build it. After the Warning, in response to the Warning, they will decide to build the Third Temple of Jerusalem, but it will take a number of years to build (about seven years). It will incorporate the Wailing Wall, and will necessitate the destruction of the Dome of the Rock Mosque.

Next, years later, the Catholic Church will build a chief place of worship in Jerusalem, a new great Basilica, which will become the center of worship for the Church worldwide. (The center of authority in the Church will move from Rome during the first part of the tribulation, to Washington D.C., but will return to Rome in the year 2040.) This Basilica will most likely be built during, and be completed soon after, the first part of the tribulation.

Lastly, an important Mosque will be built at Jerusalem, finally replacing the Dome of the Rock Mosque, but in another location. The Mosque will not be built until after 2040. So the building of the three places of worship in Jerusalem will be in the same order as the establishment of the three religions.

After the first part of the tribulation culminates with the Three Days of Darkness in late March of 2040 A.D., then Catholic Christianity, Judaism, and Islam will be the only religions on earth. No other religion will have any significant following, other than Catholic Christianity, Judaism, and Islam. There will be few, if any, persons who are Buddhists, or Hindus, or other popular religions of the present. And Catholicism will be, by far, the most prevalent religion in that future time. Judaism will be a distant second, and moderate peaceful Islam will be a more distant third.

Group Reactions: Families

Some families will be torn apart, because some family members accepted repentance and conversion, changing their lives very substantially, while other family members refused to repent and to change. Many marriages will break apart for the same reason: the one spouse repented, and the other did not. Subsequently, each will find it difficult to tolerate the other.

Some persons will be rejected by their peers, for being a good person among unrepentant sinners, or vice versa. Some circles of friends will fall apart because of different reactions to the Warning. Some groups of persons who committed mortal sins together will no longer be able to stand the sight of each another, because it will remind them of their sins.

Children will generally accept the Warning and benefit from it greatly. In this way, God will prepare them for the difficult years ahead, and build a holy generation to live after the end of the first part of the tribulation. Prenatals in the womb will benefit from this experience, being given grace to assist in avoiding sin in the future (but they will not be sinless).

The Warning will be particularly difficult for those who have willingly had an abortion, or who encouraged others to have an abortion. These persons will realize the horror of their own decisions to end an innocent human life. They will be nearly inconsolable.

Group Reactions: Businesses

Many people will be so upset and confused by the Warning, that they will not go into work for days or longer. Some will quit their jobs because they realize that immorality is part of their work, or because they cannot face their co-workers due to past sins, or because they have lost hope. The unrepentant will fare much worse than the repentant in this regard.

Many of the repentant will suddenly realize that they are in the wrong profession. Many persons who go to work in the days after the Warning will soon quit their jobs, because their lives have changed so dramatically. The result will be a great upheaval in businesses.

Many persons will be seeking new jobs. Many jobs will be left vacant because so many persons died at the time of the Warning. Many jobs will be left vacant because many persons stop going to work in response to the Warning. Commerce and travel will be greatly disrupted.

Group Reactions: non-Catholics

The Warning will not immediately cause all Protestants to realize that Catholicism is the truest form of Christianity. However, many will begin to feel an attraction to the Catholic Church and a call from God to convert to Catholicism. Some will convert at this time. But generally, at first, the repentant Protestants will follow their own denomination's teachings, and especially the teachings of the Bible, more fervently. However, the Warning is like a seed planted in fertile soil (the Protestant faithful), which will soon grow and blossom to bring about the repentance and conversion of all the Protestant Churches (in the late 2010's), and the unification of all Christian Churches in one holy Catholic Church (in the early 2020's).

The Eastern Orthodox Christians will not all immediately realize that Catholicism is the truest form of Christianity, even truer than the Orthodox faith. But some will convert at this time, and the Orthodox Churches will quickly begin to move toward later unification with the Catholic Church (in the early 2020's).

The Jews who are devout and repentant will seek to be better Jews and better worshipers of God. Jews who are repentant will tend to favor the more conservative schools of thought within Judaism. Jews who practice the faith only nominally will be strongly rebuked by God at the Warning; some will repent and begin to practice their faith; others will fall away.

The Muslims who are devout and sincere in seeking God will accept repentance and conversion, becoming holier worshipers of God. They will not generally change to Christianity as a result of the Warning. But their respect for Jesus and Mary will deepen. Muslims who are not devout, but who merely use Islam as an excuse for violence, if they do not repent with great sorrow and penance, will become very much more sinful and more prone to violence. As a result, there will be conflict between the devout moderate Muslims and the violent extremist Muslims.

Atheists and agnostics will realize that God exists. Persons who have forgotten or stopped caring that there is a God (because they have immersed themselves in the secular world) will realize the importance of worshipping God. The sin of not worshipping God is one of the main sins about which the Warning will accuse the conscience of humanity.

Some persons will try to fool themselves and others by attempting to explain away what happened. Some will offer absurd explanations. Some will seek explanations from science, from a 'new age' type spirituality, from psychology, from almost any source that will offer them the pretense of an explanation to calm

2

their fears. But everyone will know in their hearts, in truth, that there is a God and that He acted on this day.

United States Politics

Formerly, I wrote that Hillary Clinton would become U.S. President prior to the Warning. I was mistaken in this prediction. But my eschatology is speculative, and my predictions are not prophecies, but conclusions based on study and interpretation. Currently, Hillary Clinton is well-positioned politically to seek and obtain the nomination of the Democratic party for the 2016 Presidential election. But that election is held after the Warning.

Scripture does hint at a number of prominent female world leaders during the first part of the tribulation. But I cannot thereby conclude that any particular woman will be President. In any case, I expect the Warning to have severe effects on politics in the U.S. and worldwide.

I have concluded, from my interpretation of Sacred Scripture, that there will be many women political leaders during this time period of the first part of the tribulation. There are indications of this is in the book of Daniel:

{7:4} The first was like a lioness and had the wings of an eagle. I watched as its wings were plucked off, and it was raised from the earth and stood on its feet like a man, and the heart of a man was given to it.

This verse describes the transition from the politics of the U.S. and other Western nations to the politics of the kingdom of the great Catholic monarch. The group of nations allied together (for World Wars 3 and 4), represented by the lioness with the wings of an eagle, are the U.S. and allies. This figure is female (a lioness) because there will be many women in prominent political positions at this time.

But after the first part of the tribulation, when the great Catholic monarch begins to reign, political leadership will be almost entirely in the hands of men, not women. There will be much sharper and clearer distinctions between the roles of men and the roles of women in the Church and in the holy kingdom of the great Catholic monarch during the brief time of holiness and peace after the first part of the tribulation. (Sacred Scripture says that the wings of the eagle are plucked off, meaning that the U.S. will not be part of the kingdom of the great monarch.)

{8:5} And I understood, and behold, a he-goat among she-goats came from the West above the face of the entire earth, and he did not touch the ground. Furthermore, the he-goat had a preeminent horn between his eyes.

The great Catholic monarch is called the 'he-goat among she-goats' (in Latin: hircus caprarum) because he rises to power during the first part of the tribulation, when there are many women leaders among the nations that join with him to free Europe from the occupation. The above quoted verse describes the start of World War 4, in which the great Catholic monarch and his forces attack the extremist forces which occupy Europe and which threaten the rest of the world. The U.S. will provide the main military force that will attack the extremist occupiers in World War 4.

The Pro-Life Cause

The Warning will be a great help to the pro-life cause in U.S. politics. But there will still be many persons who support legalized abortion. We should expect that the merciful grace of God at this time will be accompanied by His merciful providence. One way that God's providence might work to help our nation move to become pro-life in constitution and law, as well as in heart and mind, is to bring a leader to prominence who could convincingly appeal to liberals and to women so that they would support a pro-life political position.

Hillary Clinton is a woman with a long history of liberal politics and of supporting abortion. She is former first Lady, former Senator, and now the former Secretary of State. She could make a convincing appeal to women and to liberals to change their minds on abortion. And this is the primary reason that I formerly thought she might become U.S. President. If she becomes President after the Warning, she might well take up the role of outlawing abortion. For after the Warning, the majority of U.S. citizens will oppose legalized abortion.

More About Politics

In any case, there will certainly be a great political upheaval in politics around the world, including in the U.S., at this time. The Warning will result in some political leaders dying of shock at seeing their sins, in some few committing suicide, and in many resigning from office. Many other politicians will no longer be able to be reelected, or to obtain the support of their peers, due to their past sins, and past or present sinful positions, on issues (such as abortion). The political landscape in the U.S., nationally and locally, and in nations around the world, will change suddenly and substantially, with long-lasting effects.

Most nations will become pro-life, in other words, a majority of their citizens will turn against abortion because of the Warning. If some few nations fail to achieve this advancement in morality (by becoming a nation where most citizens are pro-life), then woe to those nations! They will soon be severely punished, for the tribulation is about to begin! God is forbearing and forgiving. And so it might seem as if God does not punish nations for sin, since He lengthens the time for repentance and for reform to a great extent. But in truth God does punish sins in this life and in the next. And the tribulation is a time of punishment for sin.

After the Warning, there will be an attempted backlash against those who sincerely repented, especially against devout Catholics. Some persons in the media will attempt to ridicule or explain away the Warning, even though they themselves experienced it.

Others will attempt to blame the Church and the faithful. Those Catholics who understand the Warning will be blamed for the Warning, as if they had caused it. But such a large number of persons will accept this gift of repentance that they will not succeed in this attempted persecution of the devout faithful.

Some prominent persons and some ordinary persons will feign repentance, and some will even feign conversion, when they see that so many persons have repented and converted. Some politicians, some celebrities, some news and media personalities, and some religious leaders will feign repentance, even though, inwardly, they will have rejected this gift from God, turning away from good and toward evil. Beware of false repentance in those days!

Politicians will change their stance on various issues related to morality, some out of true repentance and some out of political expediency, since they will see that most voters are now against certain types of immorality. Beware of wolves in sheep's clothing, in the world and in the Church. Some Church leaders, including a small number of Bishops and Cardinals, will feign repentance so as not to lose power and their role in the Church. Some false prophets and some insincere evangelists will also feign repentance. Some Catholic authors, bloggers, and speakers will likewise feign repentance. Beware of persons who use their supposed conversion at the time of the Warning as a means of self-promotion.

Just as most citizens in most nations will turn against abortion, realizing that it is a serious offense against God, so also will most citizens of most nations turn against homosexuality and various kinds of sexual immorality, realizing that these are serious offenses against God. The current tide of support for same-sex marriage will be turned back by the Warning. If some few nations fail to achieve this advancement in morality (by becoming a nation where most citizens acknowledge the disorder and sinfulness of homosexuality and of all kinds of sexual immorality), then woe to those nations! They will soon be severely punished, for the tribulation is about to begin!

The World in General

The influence of the Warning on future world events is incalculable.

The Warning will bring many good people closer to God, and will bring even great sinners to great repentance. It will also cause those who reject its gift of repentance to move away from God. To reject the gift of repentance on the day of the Warning is to reject God. A significant number of persons in the world will become more evil than ever before by rejecting this gift. There will be a greater disparity between those who are holy, who seek God sincerely, and those who do whatever evil pleases them. This polarization will cause conflicts in families, in organizations, in businesses, in nations, and in the world.

The Warning will also throw the world into a great fear. The vast majority of both good and bad persons will be caught unaware by this event, even though it will be announced in advance. Many persons will be surprised and frightened by this event and by the depth of its penetration into their conscience and soul. Many persons will be terrified because their own sins have been laid bare. This confusion will be evident worldwide. Wicked persons in particular will be very afraid, knowing that their sins have been exposed and rejected by God, knowing that they have chosen sin over God. But the faithful who were always seeking to do what is good and to avoid doing what is evil, these will find not only true sorrow for sin, but also peace and advancement in holiness.

This worldwide fear will calm somewhat with the day of Consolation. But that gift is only given to those who accepted the earlier event of the Warning. Those who are unrepentant will not receive the Consolation, and so they will be more confused and more afraid than ever before at this next event. (For more on the Day of Consolation, see the chapter on the second secret of Medjugorje.)

False Prophets

Many false prophets will continue their false preaching, even after the Warning. There are quite a few false prophets today who are preaching about the Warning, but with numerous distortions and errors. After the Warning, many devout persons will more clearly discern the false prophets from the true ones. But many of the false prophets, especially the worst ones, will attempt to continue their false preaching. They will say that the Warning is a fulfillment of their prophecy, even though they stole the idea from Garabandal and then distorted it. They will try to use the Warning to promote their false ideas.

Some of the errors that they will promote at this time are as follows:

Some false prophets will claim that now is a time of peace and holiness for the world, because repentance has resulted in the sufferings that God had planned being delayed or taken away. But this is not true. Soon there will be war and great afflictions, one after another after another, for many years. I say again: some false prophets will tell you, at the time of the Warning (the Day of Repentance) and at the time of the Day of Consolation, that a time for peace has now arrived or will soon arrive. This claim is false; instead there will be war upon war, affliction upon affliction, year upon year.

Some false prophets already claim that now is the end of the world, and that the Antichrist is in the world, ready to work his evil. But this is not true. The Antichrist is NOT in the world today; his time is not until the distant future. And the so-called end of the world is very many years in the future also. So, when the Warning occurs, they will try to use that event to claim that the time has now arrived for all their various erroneous prophecies to begin. They will still continue to fool some of the weak and misguided in the world. But then, as the true events of the secrets, and of the first part of the tribulation in general, unfold before everyone's eyes, it will become clearer and clearer that their prophecies, and their messages, and their apparitions, and their signs and wonders are from devils.

Some false prophets will claim that the Warning is the fulfillment of their own prophecies, as if it proved that they are true prophets, instead of false ones. But if these false prophets mentioned the Warning previously, it was only because they stole the idea from Garabandal or from other true private revelations or from my work in eschatology. They never gave a single message that contained any specific information, other than errors and what was already known. They make only vague and uninformative predictions of natural disasters and of various types of events that are bound to occur from time to time and from place to place.

Beware of false prophets, who might try to steal information from my books about the future, and then claim the same ideas as messages from Heaven, either telling the same information (as if they had now predicted it), or pretending to make inane and useless corrections, or meaningless amplifications, of this information. One particular author has already plagiarized large portions of my eschatology, including specific dates for the Warning, Consolation, Miracle, and dates for events during the tribulation, and my description of events during the tribulation. His claimed private revelation is false, and his theft of my ideas is sinful. He has distorted and misunderstood many points within Catholic eschatology.

Peace to You

Beware of false prophets, but listen to true ones. "Do not be afraid, little flock; for it has pleased your Father to give you the kingdom." (Lk 12:32). Be ever more peaceful in your souls. With trust in God, these events will not disturb you.

2. The Miracle of Garabandal

Please understand that my writings about the future are speculative eschatology, based on study and interpretation, not based on knowledge that is absolute or certain.

At Garabandal, the Blessed Virgin Mary revealed the future events called the Warning and the Miracle. I believe that the Warning is the same as the first secret of Medjugorje, and the Miracle is the same as the third secret.

The Consolation on Easter Sunday, March 27 of 2016 (two days after the Warning) was not mentioned at Garabandal. But I believe that this event is the second secret of Medjugorje. See the later chapter on that subject. For now, let's discuss the Miracle predicted at Garabandal.

The Timing of the Miracle

Year: 2016
Month and Day: Thursday, May 12th
Liturgical Calendar: vigil of our Lady of Fatima
Time of Day: 8:30 p.m. (Garabandal time)

I understand the Miracle of Garabandal to be the same as the third secret of Medjugorje. I have termed this event The Day of Healing. The identification of the Miracle of Garabandal with the third secret of Medjugorje is my own understanding. None of the visionaries at either location have stated this concurrence.

The Miracle of Garabandal is a three-fold event:

(1) the worldwide healings of very many persons,
(2) Permanent Signs at many places of true apparitions,
(3) and the conversion of very many unbelievers.

The Miracle is the last of a set of three blessed events (Warning, Consolation, Miracle) which will refresh the Church and the world in preparation for the tribulation and its severe afflictions. Although many persons will think, after receiving these three Blessings, that a time of peace must follow, instead the tribulation falls upon the world -- because so many persons rejected the call to repentance, and some who repented, later relapsed into grave sin.

The date of the Miracle is important to my determination of the dates of the Warning and the Consolation. The Blessed Virgin Mary said that the Miracle could occur on the feast day of a young martyr of the Eucharist. And the visionary Conchita said that the miracle would NOT coincide with a feast day of our Lord or our Lady. After searching through many Saints' and martyrs' lives, I found that the best fit for the young martyr of the Eucharist is Blessed Imelda Lambertini. But her feast day is May 13th, the feast of our Lady of Fatima. Also, in some years, May 13th is the Feast of the Ascension of Jesus Christ. So that day would seem to be excluded, since it is the feast day of Mary or Jesus, depending on the year.

However, the feast day of a Saint or Blessed is usually the day of their death. Blessed Imelda died on May 12th, but since her death occurred on the day before the Feast of the Ascension (May 13th that year), at the end of the vigil Mass for that Feast, her feast day is celebrated on May 13th. So either May 12th or May 13th could be interpreted as the day of her feast.

However, according to Conchita, the Miracle will occur at about 8:30 in the evening at Garabandal. A date of May 12th in the evening can be considered to be the feast day of Blessed Imelda, since she died on the 12th of May, but at the vigil Mass for the 13th of May. Given that May 12th (of 2016) is not a feast day of Jesus or Mary, this date is fitting. It is the feast day of Blessed Imelda, and that evening (which is when the Miracle occurs at Garabandal) is the vigil of the feast of our Lady of Fatima.

May 12th does not coincide with a Thursday again (after 2016) until 2022. As I explained in the previous chapter, that date is too late to be the date for the Miracle. So the year 2016 is the best fit for the date of the Miracle. And this implies that the Warning and Consolation occur also in that year, 2016.

Like the Warning and the Consolation, the Miracle is a blessing from God intended to strengthen the Church and all persons of good will for the first part of the tribulation. At the point in time when the Miracle occurs, the afflictions of the first part of the tribulation will be imminent and will begin in the same calendar year, 2016.

The reason for the relatively brief length of time from the Warning to the Miracle is so that people can reform their lives. It is not enough for you to repent at the first secret and to accept consolation from God at the second secret. You must continue along this same path to Heaven, continually repenting, continually converting, continually striving to imitate Christ. The time from the Warning to the Miracle (49 days, inclusive; 7 weeks) is a time for people to reform their lives, to move away from sin, to pray, to practice self-denial, and to do works of mercy for persons in need (and there shall be great need during that time, especially spiritual need).

It is interesting to note that, in the Jewish calendar, in 2016, March 23rd is the Fast of Esther, March 24th is Purim, and March 25th is Shushan Purim, a celebration of Purim in Jerusalem. Then May 12th is Israeli Independence Day.

The Miracle: When it will occur

The Virgin Mary said that the Miracle will occur on a Thursday, about 8:30 p.m. (Garabandal time) on the feast day of a young martyr of the Eucharist, on a day coinciding with an event in the Church. Conchita has said that this martyr is not Jesus or Mary.

> Conchita has said: "It will happen between the months of February and July and it will be between the 7th and the 17th, but I will not tell you which year."[13]

Now some persons have claimed that the Miracle will happen in April. They drew this conclusion by putting together a series of different comments that Conchita allegedly made over the years, even though she expressly chose not to reveal the exact month. In my opinion, they drew an incorrect conclusion. What they fail to realize is that the field of eschatology includes many assertions about the future, from reliable sources, which cannot be reconciled with one another; it is not possible for all of these reliable assertions to be true. Sometimes an assertion is true if properly interpreted. Other times even Saints and other holy persons drew incorrect conclusions about the future; some of their assertions are simply wrong. So we cannot conclude, based on a set of alleged comments by Conchita, which we have only second or third hand (not directly from her) that the month of the Miracle is April. She may have misspoken, and then been unable to correct her error without revealing what she cannot yet reveal. Or she may have been misunderstood or misquoted.

I remain firmly convinced that the martyr of the Eucharist is Blessed Imelda Lambertini. I identified her as the martyr in the secrets of Garabandal many years ago, through my work in eschatology. But now I find that Pope Francis seems to have a particular affinity for Blessed Imelda. He has mentioned her in public comments repeatedly.[14] And he is the Pope who will be in office at the time of the Miracle on her feast day in 2016.

Blessed Imelda was more of a martyr of the Eucharist than any other Saint or Blessed, because she died solely due to her intense love for the Eucharist. The cause of her death was not someone killing her while she defended the Eucharist, nor was it someone killing her because she was a Christian (as in other martyrdoms). She died at the tender age of eleven upon receiving her first Communion. She went into such a state of ecstasy, out of love for Christ present in the Eucharist, that her soul separated from her body, causing her death (this can only occur when God wills it). Before her first and only Communion, Blessed Imelda prophesied her own death, saying: "Tell me, can anyone receive Jesus into his heart and not die?"[15]

She died at age 11 upon receiving her first Communion on the morning of the vigil (May 12th) of the Feast of the Ascension (May 13th, 1333). She was not supposed to receive her first Communion at that time, because she was too young. But, as she was in prayer before the Eucharist on May 12th, a miraculous light from Heaven shone down upon her, and a heavenly host was seen suspended in the light above her head, and so the chaplain wisely chose to give first Communion to her. She then went into a mystical ecstasy and died out of love for Jesus in the Eucharist. She has been named patroness of first communicants by Pope Saint Pius X.

Here is a list of reasons why she is the martyr of the Eucharist mentioned in the messages of Garabandal:

1. She was martyred as an 11 year old girl; the visionaries of Garabandal were all girls of about 11 or 12 years of age at the time of the apparitions.

2. She is perhaps the greatest martyr of the Eucharist, not including the Blessed Virgin Mary, having died purely out of devotion to the Sacrament.

3. Her feast day falls within the months and days given by Conchita.

4. The Miracle occurs on a Thursday. In the year 2016, the day of her death (May 12th) coincides with a Thursday. But the Miracle occurs in the evening, placing the event effectively also on the vigil for Friday, May 13th, the day of her official feast day.

5. Her death on the vigil of the Feast of the Ascension (in 1333), as a martyr for the Eucharist, shows us that, even though Christ ascended to Heaven on that day, He still remains with us in the Eucharist. The Miracle also is a sign of the same idea, that Christ is still present among us, though He sits at the right hand of the Father in Heaven.

6. Though she died on May 12th, her feast day is May 13th, the same day as the first apparition of the Virgin Mary at Fatima. The Miracle occurs in the evening, on the vigil of our Lady of Fatima feast day.

7. She died in 1333, a mystical number which indicates the Most Holy Trinity (three yet one).

8. Her feast day is on May 13th, again indicating the Trinity as three yet one. The day of the Miracle is on the vigil for May 13th.

9. Her martyrdom and her feast day are related to the martyrdom and feast day of St. Tarsicius, whom Conchita saw in a vision (see below, "Vision of a Martyr").

10. She is the patroness of fervent first Communions, meaning that the Church has given her a special role concerning the Eucharist. This choice by the Church also indicates that she is the martyr of the Eucharist.

11. According to an article in Garabandal Magazine, the Pines at Garabandal were planted to commemorate the first communions of children; Blessed Imelda is the patroness of first communions.[16]

Vision of a Martyr

This is an account of a vision received by Conchita on the subject of the date of the Miracle of Garabandal:

> Conchita: "The Miracle will be on the feast day of a young martyr of the Eucharist, a boy who carried Communion to persecuted Christians. His companions, on seeing him pass by, wanted to force him to stay and take part in their games. Infuriated by his resistance, they ended up hurling stones at him until he was left almost dead. Later a Christian soldier came, who recognized him and carried him in his arms."

One of those present exclaimed: "Oh, that's St. Tarcisius!"[17]

Conchita made the above statement based on a vision that she was given. But she apparently was not given a message in words, only the image of a vision. She understood that the vision pertained to the date of the Miracle. And the vision that she describes is the martyrdom of St. Tarcisius. But the feast of St. Tarcisius is in August, and Conchita has plainly publicly repeatedly stated that the Miracle occurs in March, April, or May. (Originally, she said it would happen between February and July, but later she narrowed the rage of dates.)

This apparent contradiction is not surprising. True private revelations from God are always subject to interpretation. God has wisely ordained that true private revelations be subject to possible misinterpretation by the recipient of the revelation, so that private revelation would not replace Sacred Tradition, Sacred Scripture, and the teachings of the Magisterium. Thus God was not telling Conchita or us who the martyr of the Eucharist is, on whose feast day the Miracle would occur. Instead He was giving an indication, requiring interpretation, which points to the martyr and the date of the Miracle. Otherwise, why even show her a martyr, why not just permit her to reveal the date?

So here is my understanding of the meaning of this vision:

St. Tarcisius and Blessed Imelda both died as martyrs of the Eucharist and both at about the same age. He is patron of First Communicants, and she is patroness of First Communicants. His feast day coincides with the Assumption (August 15th) every year, and her feast day coincides with the Ascension (a moveable feast) in some years. Notice the strong connection between these two martyrs. Conchita was shown his martyrdom as a way of pointing toward her martyrdom.

You have all read Sacred Scripture. You know that many truths are placed in Sacred Scripture in an obscure and hidden manner.

So, too, Conchita was shown the one martyr of the Eucharist as a way of pointing to the other martyr of the Eucharist. The Virgin Mary often presents truths in a hidden manner, requiring both faith and wisdom to fully understand.

I believe that, after the Miracle, the date for the feast of St. Tarcisius will be moved to that of Blessed Imelda, who will also eventually be canonized as a Saint, since she was chosen by Mary for this event. The Miracle has three aspects: worldwide healings, conversion of unbelievers, and permanent miraculous signs. All of these aspects will bring many conversions, will bring many persons to the Eucharist, and therefore will bring about very many new First Communions (of children and adults). So it will be fitting to have both Saints, who are patron and patroness of First Communicants, be remembered on the same day, the day of the Miracle.

An Event in the Church

Conchita has said that the Miracle will coincide with an event in the Church, one that has happened a few times in the past, but not since Conchita was born (she was born in 1949): "It is a singular event in the Church that happens very rarely, and has never happened in my lifetime.... It will happen on the same day as the Miracle, but not as a consequence of the Miracle, only coincidentally."[18]

I believe that this event is the canonization of a Pope, or more likely the canonization of two Popes. Formerly, I thought that Pope John Paul II would be the Pope canonized on the day of the Miracle. But he and Pope John XXIII were canonized, on the same day, on 27 April 2014. The most likely Popes to be canonized in 2016 are Pope Paul VI (currently a Blessed) and Pope Pius XII (currently a Venerable). Pope Francis presided over the double canonization of John Paul II and John 23, so it is easy to imagine that he might choose a double canonization again.

Pius XII was consecrated a Bishop on May 13th in 1917, the same day and year as the first apparitions at Fatima. Paul VI's process for beatification began on May 11th, in 1993. But the choice of May for their respective canonizations might be simply based on the coincident timing of the completion of each process. Their canonization might occur on May 12th, the same day as the Miracle, or perhaps on the next day, since the feast day of Blessed Imelda is officially the 13th of May.

Now, as Conchita says, this event is only coincidental to the event of the Miracle. However, the date of a canonization is generally announced well in advance. So, for some persons, this may serve as a confirmation of the date of the Miracle.

Now it is true that the canonization of a Pope has occurred during the lifetime of Conchita. Pope Saint Pius X was canonized in 1954, when Conchita was a young child. But good eschatology must take account of possible errors in reliable sources. So perhaps, when Conchita stated that the rare event in the Church has not happened in her lifetime, she did not realize that Pope Pius X was canonized when she was very young. Then later, she would have been unable to correct her error, because the correction would in effect reveal the nature of the event that coincides with the Miracle.

Will There Be A World War?

In the early 1960s, the Virgin Mary spoke to Conchita about the possibility that there would be another world war.

> Conchita: "I don't know if you remember but it was being said that a world war would break out in 1962. At the time everyone was afraid including me. Then the Virgin appeared and addressing our concern said: 'Don't be afraid, there will not be another world war.' "[19]

However, this was said in the context of the fear that a world war would break out in the 1960's. So perhaps what the Virgin Mary said should be interpreted so as to exclude only a world war at that time, and not to exclude all possibility of any and all future world wars.

But even if we interpret her meaning to refer to both the near and distant future, she could not have meant that there would never again be a major war. Sacred Scripture predicts major wars for the future (e.g. Revelation 6:2; Daniel 8:4-7). And at La Salette, the Virgin Mary herself predicted major future wars:

> "France, Italy, Spain and England will be in war; blood will flow in the streets; Frenchman will fight with Frenchman, Italian with Italian; subsequently there will be a general war which will be appalling.... there will be wars until the last war, which will then be made by the ten kings of the antichrist, which kings will have all one same design and will be the only ones who will rule the world."[20]

Therefore, IF Mary was referring to the distant future when she said that there would be no world war, she could only have meant to exclude a world war that would be truly global.

My understanding is that no future war will ever involve the whole world, neither in our generation, nor even when, in the early 25th century, the Antichrist comes to power. However, World Wars 1 and 2 are still called world wars, even though they did not involve the whole world. And Scripture clearly describes extensive wars that have not yet occurred, for example: in the Book of Daniel, chapters 8 and 11, and in the Book of Revelation, the first and sixth of the Seven Seals. Therefore, there will be a war correctly called World War 3, and another war correctly called World War 4, even though these wars will not be literally worldwide in scope.

Also, in my eschatology, there will be no future world war that involves all of the superpowers (the U.S., Russia, and China). Some have suggested that such a conflict between those three superpowers would be a part of the tribulation, but nothing of the kind fits the descriptions in Sacred Scripture and in the writings of various Saints about the tribulation. No such war will occur between the U.S., China, and Russia, nor between any two of those superpowers.

The Miracle: What it is

Conchita wrote the following, in notes given to Fr. Francisco Sanchez-Ventura, about the great Miracle:

> "it will be visible to all those who are in the village and surrounding mountains ... the sick who are present will be cured and the incredulous will believe. It will be the greatest miracle that Jesus will have performed for the world. There won't be the slightest doubt that it comes from God and that it is for the good of mankind."[21]

But if this Miracle were confined to Garabandal, it would not be the greatest miracle, nor would it be truly for the whole world or for the good of all mankind. Therefore, what is said to happen at Garabandal, the curing of the sick, will happen not only there, but **throughout the world**. Many people all over the world will be suddenly and miraculously healed by God, in every nation and in every part of every nation. This will truly be the greatest miracle that Jesus has yet performed. Recall that during His Ministry, the miracles of Jesus were most often healing miracles:

[Matthew]
{8:16} And when evening arrived, they brought to him many who had demons, and he cast out the spirits with a word. And he healed all those having maladies,
{8:17} in order to fulfill what was spoken through the prophet Isaiah, saying, "He took our infirmities, and he carried away our diseases."

Conchita also said that a sign of the Miracle would remain forever in Garabandal, and that the sign would be able to be filmed or televised.[22] But again, for this Miracle to be the greatest, and for there to be no doubt that it is from God and for the good of all mankind, there must be miraculous permanent signs throughout the world.

The visionaries of Medjugorje have said that a miraculous permanent sign would be left in Medjugorje as well; this is part of the third secret of Medjugorje. So if there will be such a sign at Medjugorje, and also at Garabandal, and if this is for the whole world, then there must also be permanent signs placed at numerous sites of true private revelations throughout the world (such as Lourdes, Fatima, La Salette, etc.).

And the result of these worldwide miraculous healings, and these many miraculous permanent signs at true sites of apparitions of the Virgin Mary, will be as Conchita said: there will be no doubt that all this is from God, and so even the incredulous will believe. Therefore, I conclude that the Miracle of Garabandal will have three parts to it: (1) very many healings, (2) and very many conversions, (3) and numerous permanent signs.

The Miracle is three-fold

1. The sick and injured will be cured. Very many, but not all, sick and injured persons, even those very severely afflicted, will be healed in their bodies throughout the world.

a. Those present for the Permanent Signs

Those who are present in any location where any of the Permanent Signs are placed by God will be miraculously cured of any illness or injury, even very severe ones. There will be Permanent Signs at Garabandal, Medjugorje, and numerous other sites of true private revelation.

Those who are present will also be cured of illnesses of the soul or spirit, such as a lack of faith, or such as a spiritual obstacle to faith or holiness (e.g. if they are angry at God, or if there is a particular doctrine that they find difficult to accept, or if they have an attachment to a particular type of grave sin). Such persons will be healed in body, spirit, and soul, so that they may believe, and so that the path to holiness may be opened up. But remember, we all walk the same difficult road to Calvary.

Those present for one of the Permanent Signs will necessarily and certainly be healed, unless they are evil or are obstinately unwilling to cooperate with God's graces (for God never assaults our free will). Some few evil persons, both those openly evil and those evil but pretending to be good, who are present for one of the Permanent Signs, will drop dead by an act of God (cf. Acts 5:5 and 5:10), because they are obstinately unrepentant.

b. Those not present for the Permanent Signs

But as for those who are not present in any location where one of the Permanent Signs is placed by God, many of these will still be healed. Out of those who are not present for one of the Permanent Signs, there is no way to know in advance who will be healed and who will not be healed. Some of those healed will be holy, others will be repentant sinners. The closer you are to God, the more likely you are to be healed. But some of the faithful will not be healed, whereas some unbelievers of good will and some repentant sinful members of the Church may be healed.

If someone has accepted the gift of repentance and of true sorrow for sin on the Day of Repentance (the Warning; the first secret of Medjugorje), and has received the gift of consolation on the Day of Consolation (the second secret of Medjugorje), and has since remained on the path to God, such a one as this, having some illness or injury from which he or she needs to be healed, will be much more likely to be healed by God on the Day of Healing (the Miracle; the third secret of Medjugorje). But even some sinners who failed on those previous occasions may be healed, if they cooperate with God's grace to a full extent.

If you are afflicted with a serious illness or injury, or a serious spiritual affliction, you should try to be present at one of the locations where a Permanent Sign will be given. But beware of false prophets, who will claim that a sign will be given where they are, but it will not be given, for they and their messages are false.

2. Very many unbelievers will be converted.

The miraculous healing includes a healing of the soul and spirit, as well as the body. For conversion is a healing of the soul. Some will be converted because they are healed by God in body, spirit, and soul. Some will be converted because they are healed by God in soul (so that God removes some spiritual obstacle to their conversion). Some will be converted because they see others being miraculously healed by God. Some will be converted because they see the Permanent Sign and realize that it is of God. Some will be converted merely because they respond to God's grace with their free will, during this time of great graces.

The number and extent of these conversions and healings will be worldwide and truly astounding. Nearly everyone will know of someone (family member, distant relative, neighbor, friend, co-worker, acquaintance) who was healed miraculously by God. The number of healings will be so many that they cannot be counted.

I warn you all: Not everyone will be healed! Do your best to convert! Do penance and pray and practice self-denial and do works of mercy and accept every teaching of the Catholic Church, before this event, beginning as soon as possible! Otherwise, you may find yourself cast aside by God because of your own freely chosen obstinacy!!!

3. Numerous Permanent Signs will be left on earth at locations of true apparitions of the Virgin Mary on earth.

The Permanent Sign is something which has never before been seen on earth, which can be seen and photographed, but not touched. The Permanent Sign will be placed by God at the sites of many various true private revelations (but not all of them). These Permanent Signs will remain forever on earth. Neither the fallen angels, nor any human power, can remove these Signs. They will be irrefutable signs of the existence of God. (Future evil generations will cover them and deny their existence.) These Signs will remain until the very last day (in the very distant future), which is called Judgment Day, that is, the day of the general Resurrection of the just and the unjust. These Signs are a reminder, not only that God exists, but that He will Judge us on the last day. (This last day is many centuries in the future.)

Since the Virgin Mary made a point of choosing a date which was related to a martyr of the Eucharist, the Permanent Sign must be somehow related to the Eucharist. Certainly the Permanent Sign is not merely the Eucharist, but it must be related to the Eucharist, so that, in some way, it points out to the world the Most Blessed Sacrament, which gives life to the world.

IMPORTANT! There are many false claimed apparitions of the Virgin Mary and Jesus in the world today.

See my articles: Claims of Private Revelation: True or False?
http://www.catholicplanet.com/apparitions/

There will be NO Permanent Sign at any location associated with false claims of apparitions or messages from Jesus or Mary. Beware of false prophets who will try to encourage people to go to their sites of false private revelations, promising them many blessings if they go. But when the Miracle and Signs occur in other places, they will not occur at these false sites, and the people there will not receive the blessings promised to them by these false prophets. There will be no Miracle or Permanent Sign at any location of false private revelation. In this way, after the Permanent Signs are left on earth, it will become clearer which claimed private revelations (messages, apparitions, signs and wonders, etc.) are true and which are false.

Now certain true private revelations might not be given Permanent Signs, either because they have no location associated with the apparitions (such as those to Fr. Gobbi), or for some other reason. But beware of false private revelations which, after they do not receive a Permanent Sign, make all kinds of excuses as to why they did not receive it. Some will claim that the Permanent Signs appeared in other places, but not at their location, because 'other blessings' were given instead. Do not believe them. Their false claims of private revelation can be discerned by comparing the content of their messages to the content of Tradition, Scripture, Magisterium. Do not be led astray by their claims of various alleged signs and wonders.

Now for those of you who were not healed by God in the Great Miracle of Healing, there is a second chance for you. Some few persons will be healed by God after the Miracle, if they are repentant and prayerful and practice self-denial and are merciful to others, and if it is God's will, when they make a pilgrimage to one of the sites of the Permanent Signs. And this benefit will remain available unceasingly until the day of Judgment, at the general Resurrection.

More About The Permanent Signs

Conchita (one of the visionaries of Garabandal) has said: "A sign of the miracle, which it will be possible to film or televise, will remain forever at the pines."[23]

Garabandal is one of the locations of true private revelation where there will be a permanent sign. At Medjugorje, the Virgin Mary gave a message about the permanent sign of the third secret there, saying:

"This sign will be given for the atheists. You faithful already have signs and you have become the sign for the atheists. You faithful must not wait for the sign before you convert: convert soon. This time is a time of grace for you. When the sign comes, it will be too late. As a mother I caution you because I love you. The secrets exist. My children! Nothing is known of these now, but when they are known, it will be too late. Return to prayer, nothing is more important than this. I would like it if the Lord allowed me to reveal some of the secrets to you, but that which He is doing for you is already a Grace which is almost too much."[24]

It has also been said at Medjugorje that the permanent sign will be beautiful and indestructible, remaining until the end of the world. It will be something that has never before been in this world. The sign will be at Apparition Mountain, in Medjugorje, where Mary first appeared.

Now I do not know what the permanent sign will be; for it is not of this world and I have never received any private revelations myself. However, I believe that the permanent sign will occur at numerous other places around the world where the Virgin Mary has appeared. So in addition to being related to the Eucharist, it is probably also related to the Blessed Virgin Mary. The permanent sign of Garabandal and of Medjugorje are the same kind of sign, occurring on the same day, along with other permanent signs (of the same type) at other places of true private revelation.

The permanent sign of Garabandal is not the Miracle itself, only a sign left after the Miracle. Similarly, the permanent sign of Medjugorje is not the third secret itself, but a sign left after the third secret. The Miracle and the third secret are the very same worldwide event: miraculous healings and conversions.

The permanent sign will NOT appear at places where persons falsely claim that the Virgin Mary has appeared. There are numerous false claims of private revelation in the world today. Some of these are due to deliberate human deception, but most are due to the action of fallen angels, appearing to certain persons in the form of Jesus or Mary or other heavenly persons. The Warning will have corrected many persons who had been deceived by these false prophets. But some persons will persist in their sins of supporting these false private revelations and their false prophets. Some might even try to claim that a permanent sign will appear at the site of their false private revelations; or they might make excuses as to why such a sign will not appear at their sites. When the permanent sign occurs at the sites of numerous different true private revelations around the world, most people will lose interest in these false private revelations.

Does the Miracle occur within 12 months of the Warning?

Yes. Formerly, I interpreted the statement by Mari Loli (another of the visionaries of Garabandal) that "the Miracle and Warning are within the same year"[25] to mean that they occur within the time frame of about a year. This was a reasonable conclusion because private revelation is both fallible and subject to interpretation. Those who treat every statement in every true private revelation as if it were infallible dogma have strayed from the true Catholic Faith. As it turns out, I was mistaken in my conclusion that the Miracle occurs one year and 33 days after the Warning. My current belief is that the Warning and the Miracle occur in the same calendar year, and in the same liturgical year; the Warning occurs on Good Friday, and the Miracle occurs on the evening of May 12th, 7 weeks later (49 days, inclusive).

The visionaries have said that many people will lose their confidence in the apparitions and messages of Garabandal before these events begin.[26] It is already evident that many Catholics, even those who believe in Medjugorje, do not believe in Garabandal. But this is not the predicted falling away from belief in Garabandal. Rather, what is predicted is that many devotees will lose their trust in the apparitions at Garabandal. Formerly, I thought that this falling away would occur because the length of time between the Warning and the Miracle would be more than a year (as I used to think). But now I believe that the Warning and Miracle occur in close succession. So what could be the cause of this falling away?

One possibility is that the temporal authority of the Church will decide against the Garabandal apparitions, prior to the Warning and Miracle. This decision could come from the local Bishop, or from the Episcopal Conference of Spain (Conferencia Episcopal Española), or from the Holy See, or from the Pope himself. It seems, at the present time, that Pope Francis does not favor private revelation in Catholic devotions. He is not opposed to all private revelation, but he does not emphasize its role. I think that Pope Francis will issue some type of negative judgment for many claimed private revelations, including the true private revelations at Medjugorje and Garabandal. Most of the claimed private revelations condemned by the Pope will be false ones. There are hundreds of claimed private revelations in the world today. Most are false, according to my research and judgment. See my list at: www.catholicplanet.com/apparitions/

It will be unfortunate if, as I believe, the Pope will issue a negative judgment against Medjugorje and Garabandal. But this type of decision is changeable; it is not an irreformable dogma. The Pope can err in his prudential judgments.

The temporal authority of the Church makes judgments of the prudential order; these judgments are fallible and may be modified or nullified at a later date. Many devout Catholics misunderstand the role of the temporal authority; they mistakenly think that one should never disagree, nor act in contradiction to such decisions. But the truths of Tradition, Scripture, Magisterium are above the decisions of the temporal authority of the Church. If such an unfortunate and erroneous decision were to be issued between now and the start of these predicted events, many Catholics would fall away from belief in Garabandal and Medjugorje. To my mind, there is no other probable event that would cause devotees of both sites of apparitions to fall away to such a great extent as has been predicted by the visionaries, and in such a short space of time.

The same falling away due to a negative decision of the temporal authority will also occur concerning Medjugorje. Perhaps the Medjugorje commission will issue a negative decision on the claimed private revelation at Medjugorje. But what seems more likely to me at this time, is that Pope Francis may make the mistake of placing Medjugorje with the many false private revelations. This mistake is understandable, since the visionaries and all the adherents of any true private revelation are fallen sinners. When they do not live up to the call from Heaven in true messages from Mary or Jesus, it obscures the truth of that private revelation.

As a result, most Catholics will fall away from belief in the apparitions and messages at Garabandal and Medjugorje. I expect this to occur in the year 2015, as the time for the Warning and Miracle draws near. After the events of the Warning, Consolation, and Miracle, no person of good will could deny that this is the work of God. Recall that when Moses and Aaron did miracles before Pharaoh, even his wicked sorcerers had to admit that God was at work (Exodus 8:19).

Here is a test of both faith and wisdom. If you have both, you might morally adhere to the private revelations at both Medjugorje and Garabandal, without sin, even in the face of a rejection of those apparitions by the temporal authority of the Church. But if you are lacking in faith or wisdom, you will not know what to do, and you will not have the confidence to sustain devotion to those apparitions.

There are those Catholics who say: "Obey, obey, obey!" That's what they say when they agree with a decision of a Bishop or the Pope. But whenever the Pope or a Bishop says or does anything contrary to the thinking of these persons, they don't obey; they feel free to disagree and complain. Do not listen to them. The Church has never required absolute obedience to every decision of the Pope or the Bishops.

A faithful Catholic can disagree with an opinion of the Pope on any matter where the Magisterium has no definitive teaching. And a faithful Catholic can disagree with a decision of the temporal authority of the Pope. You do not offend God if you continue to believe in the messages of Medjugorje and Garabandal, contrary to a decision or ruling from the Pope -- as long as you do so with respectful and quiet disagreement, with love and faith and hope, and with continued faith in all the magisterial teachings of the Pope and the body of Bishops.

No Pope or Bishop requires absolute unthinking obedience to all of their decisions and rulings. The only persons who speak this way about obedience are those who have misunderstood the call of Jesus to love God above all else.

How Should We Respond?

When the Warning, Consolation, and Miracle occur, many persons will be anxious and confused. They will wonder how they should live their lives after these blessings. My understanding is that persons blessed by these three events have no new obligations before God. They have only the same obligations that all human persons always have: to love God above all else, and to love their neighbor as themselves, to follow their conscience, to seek truth, and to strive to be better persons.

Some persons might claim that, as a result of one or all of these three blessed events, they are now appointed as a prophet or a teacher or some other type of leader over others. Don't believe it. The visionaries of Fatima, Lourdes, La Salette, and other true private revelations were not called to be leaders or teachers, no more so than other faithful Catholics. And persons who received the gift of a miraculous healing, by the intercession of a Saint, even when that miracle was approved by the Vatican as part of the cause for canonization of that Saint (!!!), were not thereby given some special role in the Church. When you receive any type of gift from God, whether by a miracle or providence or grace, you should be thankful to God. But you are not thereby appointed to some special new role in the Church or the world, nor have you been given some new type of authority. Live your life, in accord with God's guidance and your prayerful understanding.

Beware of persons, after these three blessed events, who use those events to exalt themselves. A good experience at any or all of those events does NOT appoint anyone to a role of teaching or leadership over others in the Church. After the Miracle, the Church and the world will suffer much because of the tribulation. The weak in faith will seek persons who might console them in their fear and insecurity. And many sinners will come forward, sinning gravely by teaching false doctrines, in order to gain influence over that audience. Beware of wolves in sheep's clothing. They will pretend to be holy, while leading the faithful away from the teachings of Jesus and His Church.

[2 Timothy]
{4:3} For there shall be a time when they will not endure sound doctrine, but instead, according to their own desires, they will gather to themselves teachers, with itching ears,
{4:4} and certainly, they will turn their hearing away from the truth, and they will be turned toward fables.

The Chastisement of Garabandal

Three future events were predicted at Garabandal: The Warning, The Miracle, and the Chastisement. The "Consolation" is my term for an event that follows closely after the Warning, but which was not mentioned at Garabandal. See the chapter on the second secret of Medjugorje for more on that event.

In my eschatology, the Chastisement of Garabandal is the same as the event called the Three Days of Darkness. This event occurs on March 29, 30, 31 of the year 2040. I've written extensively on this event in my book: *The Three Days of Darkness and the Time of Peace.* See that work for a long discussion of the Chastisement.

3. The First Secret of Medjugorje

Please understand that my writings about the future are speculative eschatology, based on study and interpretation, not based on knowledge that is absolute or certain.

The First Secret of Medjugorje

Year: 2016
Month and Day: March 25th
Liturgical Calendar: Good Friday

The Warning is the same as the first secret of Medjugorje.

What is the First Secret?

The First Secret of Medjugorje is exactly the same as the Warning of Garabandal. It is an event I call "The Day of Repentance", when God touches each and every human soul on earth. Generally, this experience takes the form of an illumination of the conscience, revealing to each person their own sinfulness. For holy persons, and for those who have thoroughly repented from their past sins, it will take the form of true sorrow in the sufferings of Christ, and true sorrow for the sinfulness of the world. For those souls who have not yet reached the age of reason, i.e. young children, infants, and prenatals, it will take the form of grace to assist in avoiding future sins (but they will not be sinless).

Good Friday was chosen by God as the Day of Repentance so that the world would realize, while repenting in sorrow for its sins, that Jesus Christ forgives those sins through His salvific death on the Cross. Good Friday was also chosen so that the holy faithful would have true sorrow, not only because of their own sins, but because of the suffering that Jesus Christ had to endure for the sake of everyone's sins. And this day was chosen so that the world would realize that all religions are not equal, that the Christian Faith is greater than all other religions, and that Catholicism is the truest form of Christianity.

See the chapter on the Warning of Garabandal for more details about the event of the first secret in general. See below for an explanation of certain points that have long been known about the first secret.

Ten Days Before...

Mirjana, one of the visionaries of Medjugorje, said:

> "Ten days before the first secret and the second secret, I will notify Father Petar Ljubicic. He will pray and fast for seven days, and then he will announce these to the world."[27]

Since the first secret occurs on Friday, March 25th, ten days before is Tuesday, March 15th; on that day, Mirjana will tell Fr. Peter the first and second secret. Then for seven days, he will fast and pray. Then on March 22nd, three days before the first secret, he will reveal both the first and second secrets. The date when the secret is revealed to Fr. Petar (10 days before), and the date when the secret is revealed to the world (three days before), could be off by a day, depending on whether the count is inclusive of the day that the secret is revealed, and depending the time of day. For example, Mirjana might reveal the secret to Fr. Petar in the evening on Monday, March 14th, so that there are 10 whole days before the secret. Or she might reveal the secret on the 16th, counting the remainder of that day as one of the 10 days. And the same is true for the three days before. The secret could be revealed as early as the evening of March 21st (the vigil for the following day), or as late as the evening of March 22nd.

March 29, 30, 31 of the year 2040 are the dates in my eschatology for the Three Days of Darkness, which marks the end of the first part of the tribulation; it is the last of the ten secrets of Medjugorje. April 1st, 2040, is the first day after the tribulation and is Easter Sunday. The Warning on Good Friday, March 25th of 2016, marks the start of the ten secrets of Medjugorje. And so the ten secrets unfold over 24 years by the Catholic Christian liturgical calendar, beginning on Good Friday of 2016 and ending on Easter Sunday of 2040. Notice that the two most important dates in salvation history, Good Friday and Easter Sunday, figure prominently in the start and the end of the secrets. So it is clear that the secrets are part of God's plan for salvation, and not a separate set of events.

Breaking the Back of Satan

It has long been known, having been revealed by some of the visionaries, that the first secret of Medjugorje would 'break the back of Satan.' Now some persons have incorrectly worded this as 'break the power of Satan.' The reason that the Warning is correctly said only to break the back of Satan, but not to break his power entirely, is that the Warning reduces his power significantly, but does not take away his power in the world completely. If the Warning (i.e. the first secret) had been said to break the neck of Satan, that would mean the loss of nearly all his power, since those who have their necks broken become nearly powerless. But instead the figure of speech is that the first secret will 'break the back of Satan.' Thus, Satan will lose a substantial amount of power over sinners, but not all power over all sinners.

Why does he suddenly lose so much power over sinners that it can be truly said his back is broken? Because so many sinners repent so thoroughly from their many sins, thereby moving much closer to God. Even many great sinners will repent greatly. And holy persons will become holier. So Satan loses most of his influence over them, although he and the other fallen angels can still attempt to tempt sinners, and they still retain much influence over those who refuse to repent from grave sin.

Why is it not correct to say that Satan loses all power over sinners at this time? Because a significant number of persons around the world reject this gift of repentance from sin, thereby moving further away from God and thereby becoming more susceptible to the temptation and influence of Satan and other fallen angels. In fact, the complete rejection of the gift of repentance on the day of the Warning is an actual mortal sin, causing the loss of the state of grace in the soul. Far too many persons commit that grave sin on that day.

The Upheaval

It has been said that the first secret of Medjugorje involves an "upheaval" in one part of the world. This idea is not the first secret itself, but rather, one result of the first secret. The Warning (the first secret) causes changes in the world. One of those many changes is an upheaval in one area of the world. This upheaval is a political and social upheaval, whereby evil persons, enraged and terrified by this blessed act of God in the first secret, and realizing that they are in danger of quickly losing power to good persons, gather all their supporters and then fight to maintain and increase their power over one particular area of the world, an area where evil is particularly strong: the Arab/Muslim nations of the Middle East and northern Africa.

These unrepentant wicked persons, these extremists, are not true devout Muslims who sincerely worship the One God; they are not even the Arab/Muslims who are rather worldly and who seek to bring western ways to the Middle East. Many of these extremists use religion as a mere pretext for their rise to power; they are entirely insincere in their own claimed religious beliefs. They deliberately feign religious devotion. Some of these extremists might be sincere, in the sense that they believe in their own extremist version of Islam, but this does not imply that they are acting in good conscience. However, others among these extremists are very worldly, and do not offer even the pretense of being devout.

The nations involved in this upheaval are Iran and Iraq and the other Arab/Muslim nations of the Middle East and northern Africa. In those nations, when the event of the first secret occurs, many persons will repent and seek God in true sorrow for their sins, including many Muslims. However, a significant number of persons in that area of the world will instead reject this gift from God, which He does not force upon them. God shows them their own sinfulness, but in response they may freely choose to reject His gift of repentance. By rejecting so great a Mercy, they become so much more sinful than ever before, just as the Pharisees, in rejecting the true Messiah, became much more evil than they were before the Christ arrived.

These evil persons are newly spurred on by the terror of knowing their own sinfulness and by the fear that good persons might prevail in their nations. They are deeply enraged by this merciful act of God, and so they make a sudden concerted effort to increase and reinforce their power in these nations, in the Arab/Muslim nations of the Middle East and northern Africa. They act out of fear and desperation. It is an act of deliberately choosing evil over good.

As I write these words in late November of 2014 (updating my work in eschatology that dates back many years), Iran is already in the hands of extremists. Iraq is still run by a democratic government, but large areas are controlled by the extremist group called Islamic State (or ISIS or ISIL). In 2015, I expect ISIL to continue gaining territory, and to take control of Iraq and Syria as well. Some of the other Muslim nations in that region are not yet controlled by extremists. When the Warning occurs, the extremists will make a desperate grab for power in nations not yet controlled by them. In nations already controlled by extremists, they will increase and consolidate their power.

The upheaval is an event that follows closely after the Warning (the first secret). It consists of coups, insurrections, and outright war. If extremists cannot take control of a nation's political and military powers by coups or insurrections, then from those areas over which they do gain control, they will launch sudden attacks of warfare against the nations that they cannot capture internally. There will be war and battles, chaos and killings, the disorganized and desperate acts of a loosely-knit group of persons bound by their rejection of God. It is an all or nothing gamble that they are taking. And they win. They succeed in conquering all of the Arab/Muslim nations of the Middle East and northern Africa, from Iran and Iraq, throughout the Middle East (but not the holy land of Israel).

This upheaval occurs in this particular area of the world because evil is strong there. Some fallen angels offer some impetus and assistance to these evil persons, but this upheaval is very much a surprise to the fallen angels, for they did not know when this event of the first secret would occur. The upheaval is not of demonic origin, even though fallen angels generally try to encourage or cooperate with various types of evil on earth. Rather, the upheaval is the act of human persons who reject the gift of God to be sorrowful for sin and to repent, and who deliberately choose evil instead of good. They hope (against reason and faith) that gaining worldly power will keep them safe from this repentance from sin, which so threatened them to the very core of their beings.

But, of course, they are not safe from the Justice of God. The Almighty will permit them a reign for a number of years, in order to rebuke those other nations where many persons also either rejected the repentance offered by God, or, after accepting it, fell back into the same or worse sins. But, thereafter, they will be completely thrown down and defeated.

Yes, a significant number of persons worldwide will reject this gift of the first secret of Medjugorje, which is called the Warning. So while a very large number of persons will repent and become closer to God, the number who reject this gift, and so move further away from God, will also be large. If everyone were to repent on this day, then perhaps the sufferings of the tribulation would be averted or greatly reduced. But it is not to be so. Free will and the very wide acceptance of sin in the world results in a significant number of persons either rejecting this gift of repentance outright, or quickly falling away from the path of conversion and repentance afterward.

The upheaval will occur over just a few months, beginning and ending in the year 2016. It will be initiated as a result of the rejection of the Warning by many persons in that area of the world. And it will be intensified when the Miracle occurs. For then the reprobate will be even more afraid, knowing that God has helped so many good persons around the world (whom they themselves hate for their goodness) in such a powerful way: by miraculous healing.

By the end of that short period of time (the few months after the Warning and Miracle), extremists who have chosen evil over good, who use the mask of religion to cover their wickedness, will have taken power in all of the Arab/Muslim nations of the Middle East and northern Africa. Among these nations, all led by extremists, the leader of Iran and the leader of Iraq (whoever emerges as the leaders of those nations out of the upheaval) will have the most power and control and influence over the other nations of that group. A common fear of goodness and a common evil purpose will unite these nations into one group very quickly. All this occurs, quickly, in the year 2016. The upheaval will be completed before the end of the summer in 2016. Then the extremists will consolidate their power in those nations, and will immediately begin to threaten the western nations.

After the upheaval, I expect that Iraq and Syria will be completely controlled by the extremist group ISIL. One leader from that group will emerge as the head of Iraq; he will have a military background and be an Islamic extremist. Iran will remain under the control of Hassan Rouhani, the current President of Iran. But in 2015, or after the Warning in 2016, he will also take the role of Supreme Leader of Iran (a religious position). He will be both President and Supreme Leader of Iran, which is an unprecedented amount of power for an Iranian leader.

Also, by sometime in 2015, Iran will have built at least a few nuclear bombs, and they will accelerate their nuclear program to build more nukes. **Then, sometime in 2016, only weeks after the Miracle, Iran will strike New York City with a nuclear bomb,**

beginning World War 3. So the upheaval prepares for the third world war, which is the first Seal of the Seven Seals in the Book of Revelation. The first four Seals in the Book of Revelation are also the first four horsemen of the apocalypse:

1. World War 3
2. severe civil disorder and violence
3. a widespread Famine, particularly severe in wealthy nations
4. death from a variety of causes and the fear of death

The Warning, Consolation, and Miracle have a dual effect on the world. They rebuke, console, and strengthen all persons of good will, in preparation for the sufferings of the tribulation. But these three events also have a role in initiating the start of the tribulation. For the wicked reaction of the unrepentant to the Warning, Consolation, and Miracle catalyzes events in the Middle East and northern Africa, and especially in Iran and Iraq, leading to the start of World War 3, the first event of the tribulation.

Then, too, these three blessed events are also a partial cause to the ending of the first four events of the tribulation: war, civil unrest, famine, death from a variety of causes. All four of these afflictions begin to diminish within a few years, due to the blessings of the Warning, Consolation, and Miracle. These three blessed events console and strengthen the Church and the world in preparation for the initial afflictions of the tribulation. But the Church and all persons of good will (who repented from past sins) remain strengthened by these blessings. As a result, the first four events of the tribulation will end sooner, rather than later.

The upheaval predicted as part of the first secret of Medjugorje includes changes in the Catholic Church and among Protestants and Orthodox. There will be changes in leadership as well as a sharp increase in holiness and devotion. A two-fold process occurs. Many will depart from the Catholic Church and from the Christian Faith, as part of the great apostasy, because they are unrepentant from past sins. But also many repentant sinners will return to the Church, at the same time. The departure of many unrepentant sinners, and the return of many repentant sinners begins to transfigure the Church into a greater degree of holiness. The Roman Catholic Church will clarify doctrine and make changes to discipline, while welcoming repentant sinners back to the faith. Then the different Christian denominations and the Orthodox Churches will begin to reconcile with the Catholic Church. By the early 2020's, all Christians will be united in one holy Catholic Church.

4. The Second Secret of Medjugorje

Please understand that my writings about the future are speculative eschatology, based on study and interpretation, not based on knowledge that is absolute or certain.

The Timing of the Second Secret

Year: 2016
Month and Day: March 27th
Liturgical Calendar: Easter Sunday.

The second secret of Medjugorje is the Day of Consolation; it is not mentioned in the secrets of Garabandal. I would also like the reader to know that the visionaries of Medjugorje have not yet revealed what the second secret may be. It is my understanding that an event follows after the Warning, on Easter Sunday, to console those who repented at the Warning (the Day of Repentance). My understanding of the Day of Consolation is based on the insight that the Warning (first secret) heals the soul, and the Miracle (third secret) heals the body, so the second secret must heal the spirit (i.e. the mind and heart) with consolation from God.

The faithful Apostles and disciples, sorrowing over the death of Jesus Christ on Good Friday, were consoled on the first Easter Sunday by the Resurrection of Jesus Christ from the dead. Similarly, the faithful who repent on the Day of Repentance (the Warning), on Good Friday, will be consoled on the Day of Consolation, on Easter Sunday.

Reason for this timing: To console the faithful who repented on the Day of Repentance (the Warning), to heal wounds of mind and heart, to strengthen the heart and mind in preparation for the initial afflictions of the tribulation, and to console the Church in Her sorrowing over the sins of her members and the sins of the world.

Relationship to the Warning

On the Day of Repentance (the Warning), many persons will repent from their sins, but many other persons will not repent. On the subsequent Day of Consolation, only those who repented on the earlier day of Repentance will be given this gift of consolation. Those who did not repent will not receive this gift: "so that you may know how miraculously the Lord divides the Egyptians from Israel." (Ex 11:7)

The Warning (the Day of Repentance) reveals to each of us the bad things that we have done in our lives and our vices and sins only in so far as these are still on our soul (i.e. on our conscience). But the Day of Consolation reminds us that we are created by God, are made in the image of God, and are therefore good; it reminds us of the good that we have done in our lives (but it is not an illumination of the conscience, like the Warning).

Notice that the Warning is given to everyone without any exception. God loves every person and He seeks the salvation of every person. However, based on the response to God's free gifts, some persons receive additional greater gifts, and others lesser gifts, and still others nothing more at all. The Day of Consolation will be a cause for division, because the repentant receive it, but the unrepentant do not receive it. And many of them will bitterly resent not receiving it.

[2 Corinthians]
{1:7} So may our hope for you be made firm, knowing that, just as you are participants in the suffering, so also shall you be participants in the consolation.

Those who participate in the sufferings of the Warning (first secret) by sorrowing over their own sins, will next receive consolation (second secret), to alleviate their sorrows. But as for those persons who reject the gift of true sorrow and true repentance from sin on the day of the Warning, they will not receive the Consolation. For in so far as you suffer with Christ on the Day of Repentance, so shall you be consoled by Christ on the Day of Consolation. But if you reject Christ, you cannot be consoled by Him. Jesus is willing to console you, if only you would choose good over evil.

In the Biblical view, the human person is soul, spirit, and body. But in the modern (religious) view, the human person is soul and body. So then, what is the spirit? The spirit is the breath of life that exists while body and soul are united in life, and which ceases to exist when body and soul are separated at death. The spirit of the human person is the quality of being alive; it is the interaction and close cooperation of body and soul as one person. The spirit of a human person is not a thing, but a quality. When a human being dies, the spirit (the quality of being alive) ceases to exist. This interaction of body and soul is most evident in the mind and heart. For in the mind, a part of the body (the brain) works together with the soul to understand, to know, and to remember. And in the heart, body and soul work together to express will and emotion.

There are numerous passages in the Bible which refer to the human person as body, spirit, and soul:

[Genesis]
{2:7} And then the Lord God formed man from the clay of the earth, and he breathed into his face the breath of life, and man became a living soul.

[Wisdom]
{15:11} because he ignores the One who molded him, and who instilled in him a working soul, and who breathed into him a living spirit.

God molds the human body, and He gives the human person an immortal soul. The human spirit is not a third thing. It is the breath of life; it is the qualities associated with a body and soul closely united and working closely together; it includes ideas such as the mind and the heart. Although it is correct to say that the human person is body and soul, it is also correct to say that the human person is body, spirit, and soul, because the unification of body and soul produces the spirit, that is, the qualities associated with life and with the close cooperation of body and soul as one person.

[1 Thessalonians]
{5:23} And may the God of peace himself sanctify you in all things, so that your entire spirit and soul and body may be preserved without blame at the advent of our Lord Jesus Christ.

[Hebrews]
{4:12} For the Word of God is living and effective: more piercing than any two-edged sword, reaching to the division even between the soul and the spirit, even between the joints and the marrow, and so it discerns the thoughts and intentions of the heart.

[2 Corinthians]
{1:7} So may our hope for you be made firm, knowing that, just as you are participants in the suffering, so also shall you be participants in the consolation.

Those who participate in the sufferings of the Warning, by sorrowing over their own sins, will next receive consolation, to alleviate their sorrow. This gift is granted by the Mercy of God to all those who truly repent on the Day of Repentance (i.e. the Warning, which is the first secret).

The purpose of the first three secrets is to bless all the faithful, throughout the whole world, in soul, and spirit, and body, in order to prepare them for the initial afflictions of the tribulation. The Warning is a blessing on the soul; the Day of Consolation is a blessing on the spirit; the Miracle is a blessing on the body. In this way, God gives three gifts to the world, and especially to the faithful of the world, to console, prepare, and strengthen us, in soul, and spirit, and body.

The Day of Consolation

The Day of Consolation (second secret) is a day of blessings from God on the minds and hearts of all those who repented on the Day of Repentance (first secret). This blessing will have different effects depending on the uniqueness of each person. Some persons will have the blessing of the removal from their heart of some obstacle to holiness, such as a refusal to accept a truth, or a refusal to forgive someone, or a refusal to practice self-denial, or a refusal to love more fully, or an attachment to some sin. Some persons will have the blessing of a clearing of some point of confusion or misunderstanding from their mind. Some persons will have certain emotional obstacles removed from their spirits, such as a constant sadness, or an inconsolable grief, or a lack of hope, or a lack of joy and cheerfulness, or a distaste for religion or for prayer. Some persons will be cured of some kinds of mental illness. (Other kinds of mental illness will require the healing of the Miracle.) Some persons will finally understand certain truths that they had been seeking and had been unable to reach; this will not be a direct infusion of knowledge, but rather a clarification of the mind and heart which will allow new heights of love and understanding to be achieved naturally, in cooperation with grace.

But very many persons will find that the burden of true sorrow, which they accepted as a gift on the Day of Repentance, is now alleviated by the grace of God and by this gift of consolation. And holy persons who do not need to have some obstacle removed from their mind or heart will find that this day gives them a type of renewed strength of spirit, that is, a renewed resolve in the heart and an increase in the clarity of the mind, so as to more effectively know and do the will of God.

A Sign of the Future Resurrection

The general Resurrection, that is, the Resurrection of the just and the unjust on the last day, will take place in the very distant future. The First Resurrection, described in Revelation 20:4-6, will take place in the 25th century (long before the general Resurrection) shortly after Jesus Returns at the end of the second part of the tribulation. But on the day of Consolation, an event occurs as a sign to the whole world, a sign for both the repentant who also receive the gift of consolation and for the unrepentant, even though they will not receive the gift of consolation. The event is not a resurrection, but merely a sign of the future resurrection. This is similar to that sign which occurred on the first Easter Sunday:

[Matthew]
{27:52} And the tombs were opened. And many bodies of the saints, which had been sleeping, arose.
{27:53} And going out from the tombs, after his resurrection, they went into the holy city, and they appeared to many.

Exactly how this sign will be given, or exactly what form it will take, I am not certain. I am NOT saying that anyone will be resurrected from the dead on the day of consolation. I believe that this sign is more in the way of past relatives appearing to some persons as witnesses that this day of Consolation is from God and as a preparation for the eventual (in the very distant future) resurrection of each and every human person.

Ten Days Before...

Mirjana, one of the visionaries of Medjugorje , said:

> "The first two secrets will be warnings to the world, events that will occur before a visible sign is given to humanity. These will happen in my lifetime. Ten days before the first secret and the second secret, I will notify Father Petar Ljubicic. He will pray and fast for seven days, and then he will announce these to the world"[28]

Notice that she groups the first two secrets together. Also notice the specific wording: "Ten days before the first secret and the second secret...." She words it this way because the second secret happens so soon after the first secret that there are not two separate sets of ten days preparation before each of the first two secrets, nor are there two separate announcements. The first and second secrets will be announced by Fr. Petar on the same day.

I believe that the first secret will occur in 2016, on Good Friday, March 25th, and that the second secret will occur on Easter Sunday, March 27th, only two days after the first secret. So, ten days before the first secret, Mirjana will reveal both the first and second secrets to Fr. Petar. Then he will fast and pray for 7 days, and on the 7th day, Fr. Petar will announce both the first and second secrets to the world, three days before the first event (five days before the second event).

5. The Third Secret of Medjugorje

Please understand that my writings about the future are speculative eschatology, based on study and interpretation, not based on knowledge that is absolute or certain.

The Timing of the Third Secret

Year: 2016
Month and Day: Thursday, May 12th
Time: approx. 8:30 p.m. (Garabandal time)
Liturgical Calendar: the feast of Blessed Imelda Lambertini and the vigil of the feast of our Lady of Fatima

The Third Secret of Medjugorje is same as the Miracle of Garabandal. I also call this event "The Day of Healing".

What the Third Secret Is

See the chapter on the Miracle of Garabandal. In summary, the third secret consists of three things:

1. The Gift of Healing given to very many, but not all, faithful persons and repentant sinners throughout the world;

2. Permanent Signs at many, but not all, places of true private revelation throughout the world;

3. The Conversion of very many unbelievers throughout the world, because they have been healed by God in heart and mind (making it easier for them to believe), or because they know of the physical healings of other persons, or because they see or hear about the Permanent Signs.

The Extent of the Third Secret

The Miracle of Garabandal is the third secret of Medjugorje. Do you find this hard to believe? But I say more. There are numerous other places of true private revelation which also will be given Permanent Signs, just as at Garabandal, just as at Medjugorje. Allow me to appeal to your reason as well as to your faith.

The Warning affects every single soul on earth, from prenatals in the womb to the elderly, from faithful Christians to persons of other faiths, to atheists, from the very good to the very bad, and everyone in-between. And this great expansiveness of the first secret (i.e. the Warning) is due to the great expansiveness of the Mercy and Love of God. So how is it that you think the third secret is only for one or two small towns out of all the towns and cities on the face of the earth? Even if millions gather at only one or two locations, still this is so much less than the 7 billion or so persons affected by the first secret (the Warning, i.e. the Day of Repentance).

Do you not believe that God is using these events to change the whole world? So how could this third effort by God be so limited? The answer is that it cannot possibly be so limited. God is reaching out to the whole world with the first three secrets of Medjugorje, or at least all those within the whole world who are willing to respond to God's grace.

Notice also that the Warning (the Day of Repentance) is a benefit for the soul, at least for those who accept its gift by repenting and converting. And then the subsequent Day of Consolation, though not given to all persons on earth, does affect the spirit (the mind and heart) of those many persons on earth who have accepted the first gift, that of repentance from sin. These very many persons all over the world will receive Divine consolation on that day. The gift of the first secret, repentance, is offered to everyone; those who accept it are offered the gift of the next secret, consolation. Both gifts are very extensive in scope.

So how could the gift of the third secret, meant to heal the bodies of the faithful who are in need, so as to prepare them for the next set of sufferings soon to fall upon the whole world, be applied very narrowly? It cannot. It must be applied very widely (but not universally) to those in need on this Day of Healing.

And the Permanent Signs likewise must be granted to many places, as a sign of the extensive power and mercy of God. So does God give respite and healing to the souls, the spirits, and the bodies of all those throughout the world who are willing respond to His graces and gifts. So does He prepare them for the next set of sufferings in the tribulation.

Therefore, appealing to your reason as well as to your faith, I tell you that there will be many Permanent Signs in numerous places of true private revelation. So then, the whole world does not have to go to Medjugorje or to Garabandal to be present for the Permanent Sign; there will be numerous places with Permanent Signs because these are Signs for the whole world. (But beware of false claims of private revelation, telling you that they, too, will have a Permanent Sign. For there are many false prophets in the world today.)

Little Time Left

It has been said: "After the visible sign appears, those who are still alive will have little time for conversion."[29]

If you have not repented and converted after having been offered by God the gifts of the first three secrets (the Day of Repentance, the Day of Consolation, the Day of Healing), then woe to you! Your suffering will be greater in the coming afflictions that those who have turned to God for His Divine assistance. For the end times are about to begin.

The time left for conversion after the third secret, that is, after the Permanent Signs and all the miraculous healings throughout the world, is short. There is a space of time given by God after the events of the third secret, then the afflictions of the tribulation begin with World War 3, severe civil unrest, famine, and death m a variety of causes. And the sufferings of the tribulation will increase in intensity and scope as time passes. Prepare your souls!

6. The Secret of Fatima

The Third Part of the Secret of Fatima concerns the first part of the tribulation. The Vatican revealed the third part of the secret of Fatima on June 26, 2000. The Vatican web page on Fatima contains a photocopy of the handwritten original of all three parts of the secret of Fatima, the English translation of all three parts, an official commentary, and much more.

The following is an exact copy of the text of only the third part of the secret of Fatima. It is the official Vatican translation, taken directly from the Vatican web site.

"J.M.J.

"The third part of the secret revealed at the Cova da Iria-Fatima, on 13 July 1917.

"I write in obedience to you, my God, who command me to do so through his Excellency the Bishop of Leiria and through your Most Holy Mother and mine.

"After the two parts which I have already explained, at the left of Our Lady and a little above, we saw an Angel with a flaming sword in his left hand; flashing, it gave out flames that looked as though they would set the world on fire; but they died out in contact with the splendour that Our Lady radiated towards him from her right hand: pointing to the earth with his right hand, the Angel cried out in a loud voice: 'Penance, Penance, Penance!'. And we saw in an immense light that is God: 'something similar to how people appear in a mirror when they pass in front of it' a Bishop dressed in White 'we had the impression that it was the Holy Father'. Other Bishops, Priests, men and women Religious going up a steep mountain, at the top of which there was a big Cross of rough-hewn trunks as of a cork-tree with the bark; before reaching there the Holy Father passed

through a big city half in ruins and half trembling with
halting step, afflicted with pain and sorrow, he prayed
for the souls of the corpses he met on his way; having
reached the top of the mountain, on his knees at the foot
of the big Cross he was killed by a group of soldiers who
fired bullets and arrows at him, and in the same way
there died one after another the other Bishops, Priests,
men and women Religious, and various lay people of
different ranks and positions. Beneath the two arms of
the Cross there were two Angels each with a crystal
aspersorium in his hand, in which they gathered up the
blood of the Martyrs and with it sprinkled the souls that
were making their way to God.

"Tuy-3-1-1944".

Commentary on the Third Secret of Fatima

Pope Saint John Paul II has publicly stated that he believed this
part of the secret of Fatima referred, in part, to the failed attempt
on his life on May 13 of 1981. One of the apparitions at Fatima
occurred on May 13. This may well be true, in part.

However, it is clear from the text of the secret that the account of
the martyrdoms of Bishops, priests, religious, and laypersons
refers to much more than the martyrdom of one individual:

"And we saw in an immense light that is God:
'something similar to how people appear in a mirror
when they pass in front of it' a Bishop dressed in White
'we had the impression that it was the Holy Father'.
Other Bishops, Priests, men and women Religious going
up a steep mountain, at the top of which there was a big
Cross of rough-hewn trunks as of a cork-tree with the
bark; before reaching there the Holy Father passed
through a big city half in ruins and half trembling with
halting step, afflicted with pain and sorrow, he prayed
for the souls of the corpses he met on his way; having

reached the top of the mountain, on his knees at the foot of the big Cross he was killed by a group of soldiers who fired bullets and arrows at him, and in the same way there died one after another the other Bishops, Priests, men and women Religious, and various lay people of different ranks and positions. Beneath the two arms of the Cross there were two Angels each with a crystal aspersorium in his hand, in which they gathered up the blood of the Martyrs and with it sprinkled the souls that were making their way to God."

The third secret of Fatima is about the martyrdom of bishops, priests, religious, and laypersons. Some have stated this refers to past events in the Church. Certainly part of the meaning does refer to the many, many holy persons who, in the past, have suffered much and died because of their faith in Jesus Christ.

But there is still more. The third part of the secret of Fatima follows the second part, and so the events of the third part occur after the events of the second part. At the end of the second part of the secret, the Virgin Mary says: "The Holy Father will consecrate Russia to me, and she shall be converted, and a period of peace will be granted to the world." Thus, the martyrdoms described by the third secret will occur after the consecration of Russia and a period of relative peace in the world.

According to Sister Lucia (the visionary of Fatima), this act of consecration occurred on March 25, 1984. Not long afterwards, the U.S.S.R. was disbanded, and Russia became a democratic country with much greater freedom of religion than in previous decades. Russia has been consecrated. And since that time (to the present time, as I write these words in late 2014) there has been no major persecution of Christians resulting in the large number of martyrdoms described by the third part of the secret of Fatima. Therefore, the third part of the secret refers mainly to the future, not the past.

The third part of the secret of Fatima describes a great Martyrdom, which will include the martyrdom of the Pope as well as of many other Bishops, priests, religious, and laypersons. This great Martyrdom is yet to occur. The book of Revelation predicts a time of many martyrs in the Church (Rev 6:9-11). In that passage, the past martyrs of the Church ask how much longer until God judges the earth.

[Revelation]
{6:11} And white robes were given to each of them. And they were told that they should rest for a brief time, until their fellow servants and their brothers, who were to be slain even as they were slain, would be completed.

This description of the martyrs in heaven waiting for additional martyrdoms to occur on earth is the fifth seal of the seven seals from the book of Revelation. The fifth seal is a time of great Martyrdom for the Church on earth. And this is exactly what is predicted by the third part of the secret of Fatima -- a future great Martyrdom.

Notice that the third secret of Fatima states that the holy Father and the others were actually killed. But in 1981 the Pope was not killed, and this attempt on his life was not followed by the martyrdoms of many others. The third secret of Fatima also describes a city half in ruins and the Pope passing through that city just before his martyrdom. The city is Rome, for the Pope is the Bishop of Rome. As he passes through Rome, the Pope sees many corpses, and he prays for the many who have already died. After this, the Pope is martyred. But Rome is not yet half in ruins, and the Pope has not yet fled from Rome. Therefore, this martyrdom is yet to occur. The Pope described in the third secret of Fatima will die a martyr for the Faith, after the city of Rome is half in ruins, and after he flees for his life from Vatican City and from Rome.

When will this great Martyrdom of so many of the faithful occur? It occurs during and after World War 3. The Pope flees Rome and is captured by the enemy, during World War 3. Then he dies a martyr for the Faith while in captivity. The deaths of many bishops, priests, religious, and laypersons, as described in the secret of Fatima, follow after the Pope is captured and all the more so after his death and after the War.

This is one meaning of the third secret of Fatima:

When the city of Rome is half in ruins,
then the Pope will go to his martyrdom.

The City is half in ruins because of a war: World War 3. The Pope will be martyred because the Islamic extremists who began this war capture him, put him on trial, blind him (putting out his eyes), and then imprison him; he dies in prison with no one to rescue him.

I believe that this Pope-martyr is the next Pope after Pope Francis. My prediction is that this Pope will be Cardinal Arinze, who will take the name Pope Pius XIII. The reign of Pope Francis ends perhaps as early as mid- to late-2016. Pope Pius XIII is captured during the war perhaps as early as 2017 or 2018. He dies after his capture, while he is imprisoned in Iraq. World War 3, which is the fourth secret of Medjugorje, is from 2016 to 2019 or early 2020.

After describing the martyrdom of the Pope, the secret of Fatima describes the martyrdoms of other bishops, priests, religious, and laypersons. Therefore, sometime after the Pope is martyred, many more faithful Christians will follow him to martyrdom. A time of great suffering and persecution for the Church will begin with the martyrdom of the Pope.

This persecution certainly occurs, to a significant extent, during World War 3, as the Islamic extremists capture territory and subjugate the Christians there. They will win World War 3, and they will capture and occupy a vast territory, including all of Europe. Then, in the 2020's, during the occupation, this persecution in the occupied lands will increase. Finally, from

107

about 2028/2029 through to the mid 2030's, the persecution becomes an unrestrained massacre of Christians in the occupied territories. This Christian Holocaust is the culmination of the Great Martyrdom predicted by the third secret of Fatima, which begins with the martyrdom of the Pope (the next Pope after Pope Francis).

In the secret of Fatima, the holy Angels take the blood of the many martyrs and sprinkle it on the many souls who are making their way to God. The meaning is that these many martyrs will help to strengthen and purify all the faithful servants of God on earth. The Church will increase in holiness and in all virtue with the help of grace obtained by the prayers and sufferings of these many martyrs.

How can the future be known with certainty when freewill decisions have not yet been made? Can this prediction of future martyrdoms be known with certainty and be inevitable? God dwells in Eternity. God is unbounded by Time, unlimited by Time, beyond the restrictions of Time and Place. From Eternity, beyond Time, God sees what we call the future as having already occurred. From our point of view, within Time, we have not yet made our future decisions. We know not what we ourselves will decide to do. We can decide as we see fit and our free will remains free. Yet from the point of view of Eternity (outside of Time) these future events and future free will decisions have already occurred. And the past cannot be changed. You yourself can know the past free will decisions that you made and yet these cannot be changed once they are past. And so it is with the future. God knows with certainty the decisions and events of our future without compromising freewill in the least because these future events are to God as the past is to us.

God is not trapped within Time wondering what will happen next. Nor does God use some special power to foresee from one point in time what will happen at a future point in time. God is present throughout all of Time and beyond Time, all at once, in a single act. For God is One Divine Eternal Act: the act of being all that

God is and of doing all that God does. God knows with certainty what will happen in the future because God exists beyond Time and throughout Time. God encompasses all things -- all times, all places, all events. Therefore, God can reveal future events through Sacred Scripture, through visions of the Virgin Mary, or through any other means He chooses, and these events can be known in advance, without compromising freewill in the least.

The second part of the secret of Fatima contains a conditional statement: if Russia is not consecrated, then bad things will happen. But the third part of the secret contains no such conditional statement. Furthermore, the third part of the secret of Fatima predicts the same great Martyrdom as is revealed in Sacred Scripture (Rev 6:9-11). Therefore, the martyrdoms predicted by the third part of the secret of Fatima cannot fail to occur.

7. The Tribulation: Dates and Events

Please understand that my writings about the future are speculative eschatology, based on study and interpretation, not based on knowledge that is absolute or certain.

In the year 2015 A.D.

The following is my opinion in speculative eschatology. The great apostasy begins when Pope Francis teaches truths from Sacred Tradition and Sacred Scripture, in contradiction to the assumptions and false conclusions of some conservative and traditionalist Catholics. He will teach that the Church possesses the authority to ordain women to the diaconate, and he will schedule the start of these ordinations for January of 2016.

Pope Francis will also teach from Divine Revelation on salvation theology, In contradiction to some conservative and traditionalist Catholics, he will teach that non-Catholic Christians can be saved without converting to Catholicism, that non-Christian believers can be saved without converting to Christianity, and that non-believers can be saved without converting to belief in God. All this is possible by the grace and mercy of God. However, not everyone will be saved. The state of grace is absolutely necessary to obtain eternal salvation.

Pope Francis might also upset conservatives and traditionalists by making some changes to discipline, such as allowing married men to become priests in the Latin Rite, and permitting some divorced and remarried persons to receive Communion. A faithful Catholic might opine that he made an imprudent or imperfect decision. But the Pope has the authority to make changes to discipline.

In October of 2015, these controversies will reach a tipping point and many conservative and traditionalist Catholics will falsely accuse Pope Francis of heresy. They will depart from communion with the Pope and the body of Bishops united to him, thereby initiating the great apostasy.

Also, sometime in 2015, it will become known that Iran has covertly manufactured weapon-grade uranium and nuclear bombs. Next, Iran will defy the sanctions and threats of the West and begin to make nuclear weapons openly.

In the year 2016 A.D.

March 25th, 2016 (Good Friday), the Day of Repentance = the Warning of Garabandal = the First Secret of Medjugorje

March 27th, 2016 (Easter Sunday), the Day of Consolation = the Second Secret of Medjugorje

May 12th, 2016 (feast of Blessed Imelda Lambertini and vigil of the Feast of our Lady of Fatima) is the Day of Healing = the Miracle of Garabandal = the Third Secret of Medjugorje

After the Warning, an upheaval occurs in the Arab/Muslim nations of the Middle East and northern Africa, which intensifies after the Miracle. The result will be control of those nations by extremists. Also, these nations will band together under the leadership of Iran and Iraq.

Iran will strike New York City with a nuclear bomb explosion in 2016 (probably in the summer). This attack is the beginning of World War 3.

From mid-2016 to 2019 or early 2020

The first four events of the tribulation unfold:

1) first Seal is also the first horseman: World War 3
2) second Seal is also the second horseman: severe civil unrest
3) third Seal is also the third horseman: widespread famine
4) fourth Seal is also the fourth horseman: death from a variety of causes (including disease epidemics) and the fear of death

World War 3 unfolds. The Arab/Muslim extremist forces attack and begin to invade Europe. The U.S. fights along with its European allies. This war is the first Seal and the first horseman. The Warning is not any Seal or horseman of the apocalypse. The Warning, Consolation, and Miracle strengthen the Church and all persons of good will beforehand, **as a preparation for the afflictions of the tribulation.**

Civil unrest, rioting, and street violence breaks out and increases. This civil violence accompanies the violence of the war, but it is much more widespread than World War 3; the civil unrest and violence spreads to nearly the whole world, especially in the cities. This civil unrest is the second horseman of the apocalypse and the second of the Seven Seals.

The great famine begins with the outbreak of War and civil unrest. It worsens after a nuclear missile strike against Rome during the War (in 2017 or 2018). This famine will be more severe in wealthy developed nations and less severe in poorer nations. It will be most severe in Europe. The great famine is the third horseman of the apocalypse and the third of the Seven Seals. The famine will end when the Protestant Churches repent, convert, and unite with the Catholic Church.

World War 3 continues. The Arab/Muslim extremist forces are unstoppable. After the nuclear strike on Rome, some nations surrender without a major battle. They fear a nuclear strike. The Allies are determined not to use nuclear weapons. The civil unrest, rioting, and criminal violence continues.

Some people begin living sinfully and self-indulgently, out of fear that their lives may be short. Death from a variety of different causes is the fourth horseman of the apocalypse and the fourth of the Seven Seals. The causes of death are mainly related to the war, the civil unrest, and the famine. These causes include major disease epidemics; the war and civil disorder and malnutrition allow diseases to spread more readily and to do more harm.

113

In the year 2019 A.D.

This year is the 2000th anniversary of the Crucifixion of Jesus Christ, which occurred in spring of A.D. 19. (See my book *Important Dates in the Lives of Jesus and Mary* for my detailed New Testament chronology.) The anniversary of Jesus' salvific death will coincide with the winding down of the first four afflictions of the tribulation: War, Civil Unrest, Famine, Death from a variety of causes. By mid-2020, the War will be over and there will be civil order and sufficient food. Disease epidemics and the fear of death will no longer disrupt society, as they had done since the War began in mid-2016.

2020 to 2023 A.D.

From mid-2020 to late 2023, the one holy Catholic Church will be restructured to accommodate the return to the Faith of the Protestant and Orthodox Churches. This start of this process coincides with the end of the famine. By the completion of this process, there will be ample food and feasting. The faithful will rejoice that almost all Christians are united in one holy Catholic and Apostolic Church.

During unification, in the year 2022, a new Pope is elected who is not a Roman Catholic: he will be from one of the new branches of the Catholic Church, a convert from Protestantism. Some conservative and traditionalist Catholics will not be pleased with him, but he is a true and valid Pope. Some conservatives and traditionalists will reject the one holy Catholic Church because they are upset at the unification of all the Christian Churches in one Church.

The Church will be restructured to have seven divisions within unity: one part for the Latin Rite, one part for the Eastern Churches, and five parts for the formerly-Protestant Churches.

In the years 2024 to 2029 A.D.

The renewed one holy Catholic and truly Apostolic Church wins many converts. The Arab/Muslims extremists, who hold much power over the occupied territories, are afraid and angry over the unification of Christians in one Church. They begin to increase the persecution of Christians in the occupied territories. The Church thrives and grows amid this persecution.

Some Catholics (not the new converts from Protestantism) are upset by the formerly-Protestant Catholics. This controversy about unification grows and is supported by some just complaints about serious errors in matters of doctrine and discipline among some of the former Protestants as well as among some of the life-long Catholics.

From mid-2028 to late 2032 A.D.

The Catholic Church holds an Ecumenical Council to reply to those who complain against the unification of the Protestant Churches with the Catholic Church. The Council decides that unification is God's will. But it also corrects many abuses of doctrine and practice found within the seven branches of the Church. The Council defines many new dogmas and resolves many doctrinal controversies.

During the Council, the Pope who called the Council dies. The Cardinals and Bishops then promptly elect a new Pope, and the Council resumes. This Pope will be the long-awaited Angelic Shepherd; he will take the name Pope Raphael (meaning 'God heals') because the Church and the world need healing from God and His Angels. I am convinced that this Pope, the Angelic Shepherd, will be Fr. Zlatko Sudac.

In the years 2029 to 2033 A.D.

The success of Christianity, amid the persecution and hardships of the tribulation and the occupation, angers the Islamic extremists who have power over the occupation. The success of the great Ecumenical Council causes them to be afraid that they will never overcome Christianity, and that Christianity will take away their power.

The fifth of the Seven Seals is the great martyrdom from about 2029 to the mid 2030's. The Arabs/Muslim extremists who have power over the occupied territories increase their persecution of Christians until it is no longer a persecution, but a massacre. As the Holocaust was to Jews, so this great Martyrdom is to Christians. Clergy and religious will be hunted down, tortured, and killed. Tens of millions of Christians in the occupied territories will be massacred. It will be the worst persecution of Christians in the history of the world.

In the years 2034 to 2037 A.D.

The massacre of Christians and the threat of a nuclear first-strike by the enemy spurs the United States and its Allies to undertake World War 4. This war is an all-out nuclear war, with the Allies making the first strike (using pure fusion weapons). The great Catholic monarch is the most prominent of the leaders among the Allies. The Angelic Shepherd, the very holy Pope of that time, also approves of this war.

The sixth of the Seven Seals is World War 4, an all-out nuclear war, which begins about 2033/2034 and ends about 2037 A.D. The United States uses pure fusion weapons, but the extremist forces use older fission-fusion weapons.

The army of the great Catholic monarch is small, but they call upon the intercession of the Virgin Mary, and the help of the holy Angels, so they are able to defeat a much larger force. The occupying forces are defeated in both the occupied lands and in their own lands.

After, or near the end of, this war, some of the faithful are given the Seal of God on their foreheads, a visible sign of the favor of God, along with great interior gifts.

The great Catholic monarch and the Angelic Shepherd survive the war. The faithful want the great Catholic monarch to rule over the entire territory formerly held by the Arab/Muslim extremist forces. But the politicians and the media oppose and ridicule this idea. They manage to convince people not to approve of this idea. But then...

In the years 2038 A.D. to early 2040 A.D.

The Seventh Seal is divided into seven additional sets of events, symbolized by trumpets.

The First Trumpet of the Seventh Seal - pieces of the broken Comet Tempel 1 fall to earth and burn up a third of the land area.

The Second Trumpet of the Seventh Seal - one large piece of Comet Tempel 1 falls into the ocean and causes great destruction worldwide.

The Third Trumpet of the Seventh Seal - nuclear fall-out from World War 4 poisons one third of the waters on earth.

The Fourth Trumpet of the Seventh Seal - nuclear winter, from World War 4, as well as from the fires caused by the broken comet, reduces the light that reaches the earth, causing crop failure, freezing temperatures, and a sudden widespread severe famine.

The Fifth Trumpet of the Seventh Seal - something similar to locusts (probably preternatural in origin) torments for five months those who do not have the Seal of God on their foreheads.

The Sixth Trumpet of the Seventh Seal - the Three Days of Darkness occurs on March 29, 30, 31 (Maundy Thursday, Good

Friday, Holy Saturday) of 2040 A.D., during which about one third of the world population will be killed. (Another one third of the world population will have been killed by all the prior afflictions of the tribulation combined.) Anyone caught outside or who goes outside, and anyone opening a window or door to the outside, during these Three Days of Darkness, will be killed. Some persons indoors will be killed by their own fear.

By the end of the Three Days of Darkness, God will have miraculously healed the world of the lingering effects of the previous afflictions. A vast number of unrepentant sinners will be dead, but those who remain will be holy and humble; they will fear and love God.

Beginning in the year 2040 A.D.

After the Three Days of Darkness, those who survive will agree to allow the great Catholic monarch to rule over the entire territory formerly occupied by the Arab/Muslim extremist forces, including Europe, parts of Eastern Europe, parts of Scandinavia, the entire Middle East, and northern Africa. Before the Three Days of Darkness, the media and various prominent persons ridiculed the idea of the great monarch ruling over a vast territory, and the idea of the three days of darkness. And they will have effectively convinced the nations not to allow it. But after the three days of darkness, those who survive agree to submit to the great Catholic monarch. The secular media have now utterly lost their power.

The great Catholic monarch begins to rule over a vast territory. His kingdom places the Catholic faith above the government of the kingdom. His constitution and laws are based on the Catholic faith. His kingdom is not perfect, but it is the holiest mere earthly kingdom that the world will ever see. But the kingdom of Jesus Christ is above and beyond all earthly kingdoms.

The Angelic Shepherd is the holy Pope of that time period: Pope Raphael. He will be able to work miracles through prayer and through the intercession of the Virgin Mary. He will teach the Faith with greater depth and insight than any previous Pope. The Catholic Faith will hold great influence with all the nations of the world.

The Church will rebuild a new Vatican City at Rome. The papacy returns to Rome in the year 2040 A.D. The center of authority in the Church will be Rome, and the center of worship in the Church will be Jerusalem. The Eastern Rite of the one holy Church will be in charge of the center of worship in Jerusalem.

In the 2040's A.D.

The afflictions of the first part of the tribulation have ended. There are very many dead bodies left from the three days of darkness, which killed one third of the world's population. It takes years for the world to locate and bury or cremate all of the dead.

The world begins a period of rebuilding and recovery. The great Catholic monarch begins his reign over the vast territory formerly held by the extremist forces. The Angelic Shepherd, the very holy Pope of that time, leads and teaches, confirming the decisions and deeds of the great Catholic monarch.

Catholicism holds great influence over all governments and peoples during this time. The governments and laws of the world are mostly formed according to the teachings of the Church and the will of the Pope. The evils found in society before the tribulation and before the three days of darkness are greatly diminished and have little influence.

Few people have electricity. Few have gasoline for vehicles. Very great destruction was done to the infrastructure of modern society during the tribulation. People live simple humble lives; they are happy to have peace and truth, food and shelter. Prayer works wonders for those who live according to the Church's teaching. And these humble persons are guiding lights to the rest of the world.

But, over the course of time, society begins to rebuild. Industry and commerce and modern conveniences begin to return.

Many persons throughout the world convert to Catholicism. The number of converts is astounding and overwhelming. Many Catholics move to Israel. The nation of Israel will be so overwhelmed by the number of persons wanting to live there, that many will find room only in neighboring nations. The nations of the Middle East and northern Africa will become the suburbs of the Holy Land. Israel will become mainly a Catholic Christian nation, but with many faithful Jews there also.

A new Vatican City will be built at Rome. And at Jerusalem, a new Catholic Christian Basilica will be built, and a new Mosque. So now the suggestion of Pope, after the Warning, that there be three places of worship in Jerusalem (a Church, a Temple, and a Mosque), reaches its fulfillment. The Third Temple of Jerusalem will be embellished; it will have survived the first part of the tribulation.

The world becomes clearly committed to three main religions: Catholic Christianity, devout Judaism, and moderate Islam. The vast majority of persons in the world will be Catholic Christian. Catholicism will be the foremost religion of the world; Judaism will be a distant second; Islam will be a more distant third.

The great Catholic monarch will rule even over the nations of the Middle East. He will build an opulent Catholic Basilica in Iran. The Catholic Church will win very many converts to Catholicism during this time. Even whole nations will convert.

In the 2050's and 2060's A.D.

The Angelic Shepherd dies, perhaps as soon as the mid to late 2040's; or perhaps as late as the 2050's. The great Catholic monarch continues to reign. The next Pope after the Angelic

Shepherd is also very holy, and also takes the name of an angel (as do his immediate successors).

The world is now beginning to forget the afflictions of the tribulation. Modern technology is returning at an ever increasing rate. Catholicism still has much influence over the leaders of the world, but the social ills of the not-so-distant past are straining to reassert themselves. By 2066, the secularism and errors of the past will have gained a sure foothold. But first Catholicism spreads widely. For many years, even after the brief time of peace and holiness, Catholicism continues to be first among all religions on earth.

The great Catholic monarch willingly lays down his crown at Jerusalem, resigning as leader of the vast territory formerly held by the Arab/Muslim extremist forces. The impious influences of the world, which were straining under the holy rule of the great Catholic monarch, fear another pious leader will replace him. They use the media and every tool of influence at their disposal to prevent this from happening. They appeal to regional self-interest and to impious desires. They appeal to a false idea of freedom and autonomy. They do not want Catholicism to rule over them. They succeed in convincing a majority of persons that the kingdom of the great Catholic monarch should be divided.

The great Catholic monarch's kingdom becomes divided into four parts, just as Scripture foretells. The North includes most of Europe. The South includes Israel, the Middle East, and the northern part of Africa. The South has become the holiest region in the world, due to the influence of Catholicism, Judaism, and Islam. There are two other smaller and less influential regions also.

At this time, some Catholics slip in to greater sinfulness, despite clear teachings of the Church to the contrary. But most of the increase in sinfulness is found in secular society. With the return of sinful living comes the return of the harm to society that comes from sin. Crimes and conflicts resume and gradually increase.

In the remainder of the 21st century

This slide toward sinfulness, and the relaxation of laws and rules, continues. Slowly, constitution and law are altered, so that greater and greater sinfulness is permitted. The news and entertainment media again begin to spread dissent and disorder and false teachings and sinfulness.

Even so, this time is one of great holiness for the Church and the faithful. The Church and the true faithful continue to increase in holiness and in knowledge of God, despite the increase in sinfulness of secular society. But not all members of the Church in this time remain faithful to Church teaching; some fall under the influence of sinful secular society.

In the 22nd, 23rd, and 24th centuries

The world becomes increasingly sinful. The Church remains pure and uncorrupted. But many of Her members fall into grave sins, due to the influence of secular society.

In the 24th century, the kingdom of the ten kings is established. This kingdom is described in the Book of Daniel and the Book of Revelation, as well as in the secrets of La Salette.

In early 25th century

The Antichrist is born in the late 24th century, and he rises to power in the early 25th century. His kingdom lasts for less than 7 years; the last half of that time (3.5 years) is the time of the greatest persecution of the Church in all of history. In the end, the Antichrist is defeated and his kingdom collapses.

Jesus Christ returns from Heaven, with the Virgin Mary, in the year 2437 A.D. They return in the sight of the whole world, neither secretly nor quietly. Jesus establishes His kingdom on earth as in Heaven. He then ascends to Heaven and the Virgin Mary is also assumed into Heaven.

The Millennium of Peace and Holiness

This time period lasts well over a thousand years, and perhaps as long as about 1,200 years:

[Song of Songs]
{8:13} *Groom:* My vineyard is before me. The thousand is for your peacefulness, and two hundred is for those who care for its fruit.

The Church on earth continues to lead the people of God, and now also governs the whole world. A time of great peace and great holiness prevails over all the earth. The martyrs and Saints of the First Resurrection, including the First Fruits, are great leaders and teachers in the Church on earth, teaching by word and by example. Their word cannot be contradicted because they have been resurrected from the dead as a confirmation of their holiness, and because they have the Beatific Vision of God continuously. They cannot err in word or in deed.

Christ is in Heaven during this time. But He reigns through the Church and the Sacraments, especially through the Eucharist. He is not physically present on earth, except in the Eucharist, during this time, because He has ascended to Heaven.

The Brief Rebellion

This rebellion occurs at the end of the Millennium, during a brief space of time, perhaps sometime between 3500 and 4000 A.D. (not for that entire length of time, but for a very brief time somewhere within that range of years). The devils are released and are once again permitted to tempt people. Although the world has been very holy for centuries, many persons freely choose evil over good. Some of these had already gone astray in their hearts; others go astray when tempted by the fallen angels.

These wicked sinners gather to make war against the Church, but there shall be no war. Instead, they are destroyed by God in response to the prayers of the faithful on earth.

[Revelation]
{20:7} And when the thousand years will have been completed, Satan shall be released from his prison, and he will go out and seduce the nations which are upon the four quarters of the earth, Gog and Magog. And he will gather them together for battle, those whose number is like the sand of the sea.
{20:8} And they climbed across the breadth of the earth, and they encompassed the camp of the Saints and the Beloved City.
{20:9} And fire from God descended from heaven and devoured them. And the devil, who seduced them, was cast into the pool of fire and sulphur,
{20:10} where both the beast and the false prophetess shall be tortured, day and night, forever and ever.

After the Millennium and the Brief Rebellion:

Jesus returns from Heaven for a second time. Then the general Resurrection of the just and the unjust occurs. All the souls from Heaven, Purgatory, and Hell are resurrected. The wicked are given horrible bodies, befitting of their sins. The just are given glorious bodies like the resurrected bodies of Jesus and Mary.

Then God takes away Heaven and Earth and Purgatory and Hell. And God makes a new Heaven and a new Earth, and a new Hell. A new Heaven is needed because the resurrected Just now have bodies and souls, not souls only. The new Heaven is fitting to body and soul. A new Hell is needed because the resurrected Unjust now have bodies and souls, not souls only. The new Hell is fitting to body and soul. The new Heaven, new Earth, and new Hell continue forever.

The resurrected Just are assumed into the new Heaven in the Assumption of the faithful. The resurrected wicked are thrown into the new Hell, where they will suffer unceasingly in both body and soul. And death is no more. And Purgatory is no more. And when God makes a new Earth, its capital will be the New Jerusalem, a city created by God, not by man.

And after that...only God knows.

Christ's Kingdom Is Without End.
Amen.

Endnotes

[1] THE THREE POPES AND GARABANDAL: Revisited Again in Light of the Passing of His Holiness Pope John Paul II; by Geoffrey A. P.Groesbeck. April 2005.
http://www.ourlady.ca/info/THE_THREE_POPES_AND_GARAB.htm

[2] NBC News, "Pope Francis: I Could Quit Like Benedict or Even Die by 2017",
http://www.nbcnews.com/news/world/pope-francis-i-could-quit-benedict-or-even-die-2017-n183721

[3] CatholicPlanet.net, "a new Pope in 2 or 3 years", 19th August 2014; See comments by OregonCatholic and myself:
http://www.catholicplanet.net/forum/showthread.php?t=5770

[4] Edward Connor, Prophecy for Today, (TAN books: Rockford, Illinois, 1984), p. 126.

[5] Edward Connor, Prophecy for Today, p. 126.

[6] Pope Saint John Paul II, Redemptoris Missio, n. 10.

[7] Pope Saint John Paul II, All Salvation Comes through Christ, General Audience, May 31, 1995.

[8] There are conflicting sources on his age. This site says he was 31 in 1961, and 33 in early 1963 (when he met Padre Pio)
http://www.garabandal.us/joey.html

[9] Garabandal magazine, special edition, 'The Warning and the Miracle,' p. 15.

[10] Garabandal magazine, special edition, 'The Warning and the Miracle,' p. 18.

[11] Garabandal magazine, special edition, 'The Warning and the Miracle,' p. 14.

[12] Garabandal magazine, 'The Warning and the Miracle,' p. 12.

[13] The Workers of Our Lady, Canada, 'Interview with Father Gustavo Morelos,' http://www.ourlady.ca/info/InterviewFrMorelos.htm

[14] National Catholic Reporter, "Pope Francis and the invocation of Blessed Imelda" by Megan Fincher, Sep. 19, 2013;
http://ncronline.org/blogs/francis-chronicles/pope-francis-and-invocation-blessed-imelda

[15] Catholic Online, Saints and Angels, 'Blessed Imelda,'
http://www.catholic.org/saints/saint.php?saint_id=125

[16] Gabriel Garnica, Oct-Dec 2004 issue of Garabandal Magazine.

[17] The Workers of Our Lady, Canada, 'With the Miracle in Sight,'
http://www.ourlady.ca/info/book3/three07e-withMiracleSight.htm

[18] Garabandal magazine, 'The Warning and the Miracle,' p. 28.

[19] The Workers of Our Lady, Canada, Interview with Bishop Garmendia,
http://www.ourlady.ca/info/conchita2.htm

[20] Abbé Combe, Curé of Diou (Allier), Le Secret de Melanie, 1904; Melanie's secret, translated by Ronald L. Conte Jr., paragraph n. 19, 23.

[21] Garabandal magazine, 'The Warning and the Miracle,' p. 6-7.

[22] Garabandal magazine, 'The Warning and the Miracle,' p. 6-7.

[23] Garabandal magazine, 'The Warning and the Miracle,' p. 7; Spanish translation of some phrases in this quote were removed.

[24] OurMedjugorje.com;
http://www.ourmedjugorje.com/The%20messages.htm

[25] Garabandal magazine, 'The Warning and the Miracle,' p. 14.

[26] The Workers of Our Lady Canada, 'The Three Phases of Garabandal,' http://www.ourlady.ca/info/threePhases.htm; see also Garabandal magazine, special edition, 'The Warning and the Miracle,' p. 10.

[27] Janice T. Connell, The Visions of the Children, p. 66.

[28] Janice T. Connell, The Visions of the Children, p. 66.

[29] Father Tomislav Vlasic's Letter to Pope John Paul II,
http://www.medjugorje.org/vlasic1.htm

17559482R00079

Made in the USA
Middletown, DE
01 February 2015